The Legacy of Eulan Brown

SpeakingDirect Publishing
Marietta, Georgia
www.speakingdirect.com
Library of Congress Control Number: 2009940417

Bruce Goddard
Author of *View From a Hearse – Lighten Up!*

The Legacy of Eulan Brown

ISBN 13: 9780976777014

Printed in the United States of America

Dedication

To Taylor and Anna Kate
This is for you and for your brothers and sisters and cousins one day who are not yet born. I hope you always remember the lessons of Eulan Brown.
And never forget your Papa.

Acknowledgements

My parents--Ed and Naia Goddard: They instilled in me a desire to make a difference and gave me an inquisitive nature to look under the superficial layers to see the best in others. I miss them every day of my life.

My wife--Kathy: My editor says I use the word "incredible" too much. There is no way I could use that word too much in describing you. You encourage me, pray for me, always give me the freedom to do what's in my heart and you pushed me to publish this book. You really are incredible, and I love you.

My three sons--David, John and Luke: I have seen you in the ditch, and I have seen you choose to gather your papers, put them back in the basket and get on down the road. You all are winners, and you make me more proud than you could ever know. There will be more ditches and more choices – life is a journey. But you know what to do.

To my three daughters-in-law--Holly, Tami and Drew: I know my boys are winners, because they married you. When I think of "squeezing" life, I think of the times we all have spent together and will spend together. Life doesn't get any better. I love all three of you just as much as I love your husbands.

To my brother-in-law--Rudy: This book would not be a reality if not for you. Period. Thank you for your time, your effort and your expertise.

Most importantly--To God: If the stories and lessons of this book cause even one person to realize their need for You, the long hours and effort to write this book and publish it would all be worthwhile.

"You are a shield around me Oh Lord; you bestow glory on me and lift up my head." *Psalms* 3:3 NIV

Contents

Basket Two: Squeezing Life

Basket Three: Winning

Basket Four: Knowing People

Foreword

By Jimmy Childre, Jr.

Bruce Goddard is a funeral director, corporate executive, humorist, author, public speaker, observer of life and God's servant. He is also my lifelong friend. We were born in September of 1954, seventeen days apart and grew up in the small town of Reynolds, right in the heart of rural Georgia. Looking back on it now, I believe we grew up in a real life Mayberry and that unique experience during our formative years laid the foundation of what was yet to come. It is this common beginning and our enduring friendship that enables me to share my view of Bruce Goddard, both the writer and the extraordinary human being.

Our families had lived in Reynolds for several generations and had businesses across the street from each other. Bruce's family owned and operated a grocery store and funeral home, while my family had a Chevrolet dealership. His father joined his grandfather's business and my father joined my grandfather's business. Later, Bruce joined his father's business, and I joined my father's business.

Across the street from our families' businesses was the church square. The square was home for the Methodist and Baptist churches, located diagonally from each other with a small park in between the two. Our families were members of the Methodist church; however, we had many friends and knew everyone in both of the churches. Actually, everyone in Reynolds knew everyone else, along with everything about them and their family's history.

To the casual observer Reynolds may not have appeared to offer much to its citizens, especially to its youth. After all, we didn't have a shopping mall, movie theaters, fast food restaurants or a recreation center. With a town population of only 1,200 people, our school wasn't large enough to field a football team. Automobile traffic was sparse and the streets were wide, so we didn't even need a traffic light. The traffic violations and the crime rate were so low that one policeman could handle the day shift and a town "night watchman" was more than adequate while we slept.

What did make Reynolds exceptional were its incredible people. First, we had an excellent school system, and it excelled in every dimension--from academics to athletics (baseball, basketball, track and field.) Reynolds High School was well known for its literary prowess, and its students frequently won both regional and state competitions. Also, the churches had an influential role in our lives and almost everyone in Reynolds was active in their church. Even though our community was small, it was filled with extraordinarily talented people and they were always giving of themselves. Each generation in Reynolds was committed to the next. Everyone wanted everyone else to succeed. Our school teachers, our little league coaches, our church leaders, our community leaders, our merchants, and our parents were all the same group of people. They always cared for us and made sure we did the right things. It was also clearly understood that wherever we were and whatever we were doing, every adult had full authority to act on behalf of our parents. While we may have lacked a few amenities in Reynolds, we had everything we needed, especially to prepare us for who we would become and what we would pursue in life.

Bruce and I started the first grade together, played little league baseball together, rode our bicycles all over town together, collected and traded baseball cards, and attended Sunday school and church together. We rode to high school together almost every day, doubled dated, joined the same clubs and even took the SAT exam together – twice. It is interesting that after the two attempts, we had exactly the same average score. One thing is for sure, we always enjoyed whatever we did together and Bruce made sure that he kept me laughing. As a matter of fact, he was the class comedian in school, and he made sure he kept everyone laughing. The combination of his light heartiness and my seriousness often positioned me to be the straight man for many of Bruce's hilarious stories and side splitting jokes.

We started playing golf at an early age because our families were founding members of the Reynolds Golf Club. Our golf course was not part of a real estate development nor was it planned by a famous designer, but it was built by those same community leaders who saw the value in our small town having such a place for families to spend time together. Bruce and I enjoyed hundreds of rounds of golf there. Our conversation on the golf course would evolve from all the things boys would normally discuss to the topics that young men begin to ponder. While we always had many laughs together on the golf course, it was during those days of walking side by side down the fairways that we began to turn toward the more serious questions of life. We contemplated the meaning of life, faith, and death. We sometimes wondered where we would live as adults and what professions we would enter.

One spring evening I answered the career question for both of us. We were in my house cleaning our golf clubs for the next day's tournament when Bruce's dad, Mr. Ed, called and instructed us to meet him at the local hospital to help transport a body to the funeral home. I was not at all comfortable with what we were about to do but I went along with it. Afterwards I was left standing in the funeral home hallway while Bruce and his dad were about to begin the next task. I told Mr. Ed that I thought my mother was calling me, and I needed to leave immediately. As I walked (maybe ran) home that night, I felt very confident that one day Bruce would join the family business. I also was completely sure of one profession that I could strike off of my list.

Bruce became a fourth generation funeral director and anyone that has ever attended a Goddard Funeral Home service will tell you that no one conducted a funeral with more reverence, compassion and professionalism than the Goddard family. Bruce later acquired another funeral home and grew the family business until he sold it to a national funeral home chain. He joined the national company and rapidly climbed the corporate ladder. Today Bruce is a very successful executive and valuable member of their management team.

The years of managing a funeral home and spending so much time with families during the most difficult times in their lives exposed Bruce to the very essence of what is important in life. He has a unique view of what really does and does not matter and combined with his sense of humor and storytelling skills, he is able to assist the rest of us in understanding our own day-to-day successes and failures.

In Bruce's first book, *View from a Hearse,* he introduces us to life in Reynolds and tells many humorous stories of his experiences with people there. He then shocks us by explaining that the world isn't going to stop when we pass away and that life will constantly present us with hardships. He suggests how to cope with the "darkness" in our lives and consequently how to fully appreciate the "daylight." *View from a Hearse* is both hilarious and provocative...in typical Bruce Goddard style.

Bruce's demanding travel schedule, for both his corporate work and his numerous public speaking engagements, offers him many opportunities to meet new people. He seems to always position himself for that unique personal encounter where he comes away touched by someone's story and then he shares it through his blogs, speeches and books. Bruce doesn't seek out the rich and famous, although from time to time he may give us an unexpected view of them. He more often sees the special qualities of the unnoticed people and then effortlessly brings them into our lives where we can benefit from the lessons learned through his observations.

In this book, Bruce compiles stories about people he has met in his travels as well as people who grew up in Reynolds. One of those people is Eulan Brown. He was physically challenged and made a very meager living selling *Grit* newspapers from his bicycle. He was always wrecking his bicycle in a ditch or against a curb, spilling the newspapers from his basket and finding himself on the ground. As young boys, we would point and laugh while he got up, gathered his newspapers, and brushed himself off in an awkward kind of way to continue on his journey. This continued day after day and year after year.

Through Bruce's God given gift of seeing what the rest of us can't see, he has written *The Legacy of Eulan Brown.* With his talent for storytelling, he uses the stories to illustrate the lessons he observed from Eulan Brown, a man that essentially went unnoticed except when he failed.

Bruce's writing and speeches have inspired thousands of people and I am confident many more are about to be inspired as a result of this book. Bruce's unique view gained from being a funeral director in the little town of Reynolds, coupled with his keen sense of humor and sincere appreciation of life formed the perfect combination for what he accomplishes in this book.

When I read these stories I am taken back to Reynolds and remember the wonderful times Bruce and I shared there. We were constantly in each other's home and I can't count the number of times I spent the night at Bruce's house. Bruce's parents, Miss Naia and Mr. Ed, were very loving and caring people and always made me feel a part of their family. Each night when I was in their home, Miss Naia made sure we came to her room so that she could hear us say our prayers. At first, I thought she was making sure we learned how to pray and that she hoped we would always practice it. I later realized that she was not only doing that, but she was also praying with us and for us.

Bruce and I were christened together when we were about six months old and he recently discovered a home movie taken right afterwards. My father is holding me and walking toward Miss Naia as she is holding Bruce. I have a very serious expression on my face as we approach them. Once we are close to each other, Bruce picks up something that is attached to his blanket as though he is showing it to me. He begins to laugh and so do I. My father has always told me people don't ever change, they just mature. I am beginning to believe him and in this case I am glad he is right.

God blessed me through my lifelong friendship with Bruce Goddard. God blessed Bruce with a special gift and He shares it with us through his moving stories. As you read this book you will laugh and cry, think about and understand what's important, and see life as God intended for us to see it.

I believe Miss Naia and Mr. Ed are looking down from Heaven and are very proud of what Bruce is doing for everyone he touches. Miss Naia's prayers were answered.

Jimmy Childre, Jr is founder and owner of Childre Ford-Mercury, Inc in Sandersville, Georgia and is Chief Executive Officer of Washington County Regional Medical Center in Sandersville. He received his Bachelor of Business Administration from Georgia Southern University and Global Master of Business Administration from Duke University. Additionally, he graduated from Harvard Business School's Owner/President Management Program and received a Master of Studies Degree from the University of Cambridge. Jimmy is a frequent guest lecturer at the Fuqua School of Business at Duke University.

The Lessons of Eulan Brown

When I was growing up in the little Georgia town of Reynolds, there was a guy who delivered *Grit* newspapers on his bicycle. I would guess that Eulan Brown was about 15 years older than me. I remember him well because I saw him almost every day riding his bicycle through the neighborhoods of Reynolds delivering his papers.

Actually most of the time I saw Eulan, he was not riding his bike. Instead his bicycle was usually on its side in the ditch and his *Grit* papers were strewn all over the ground. The mental picture I have carried with me is of Eulan picking his papers up and putting them back in his basket so he could continue on down the road.

Seemed like he was always in the ditch, gathering his papers and putting them back in the basket.

Eulan had a muscular disease, and he had a terrible time keeping his balance. In fact, my buddies and I would ride our bicycles behind Eulan and boo him and scare him. He would jerk his head around and immediately wreck his bicycle. We would all laugh and ride on down the road knowing Eulan had to get his papers back in his basket before he could continue on down the road.

One day, when I was about twelve years old, I was sitting at the lunch counter at Hicks Trussell's store in Reynolds. Mr. Trussell ran a little grocery store, but he also cooked hamburgers for the townspeople. I remember the place being crowded when I sat down on one of the stools to order my hamburger. In just a few minutes, the guy I was sitting next to finished and got up to leave. Eulan Brown sat down next to me.

I almost got up to leave. I think I was afraid of him. I had never been that close to him by myself, and he was much older than me. I considered him to be some kind of weirdo. But as soon as he sat down, he began to speak to me. He called me by name. He asked me about my mom and dad and my brothers and sister. I couldn't believe what I was hearing. He talked normally and was very nice. Even as a young kid, it began to dawn on me that day that Eulan Brown was a normal human being.

I can tell you I never laughed at Eulan Brown after that day. In fact, the next time I saw him with his papers all over the road, I stopped to help him gather his papers and get them back in the basket, so he could go on down the road.

I never forgot Eulan Brown. And I never forgot the lessons I learned from his life.

I would later realize that there would be many times in my own life that I would find myself in the ditch with my papers strewn all over the place. I would have two choices. I could spend my time moaning, groaning, complaining and wondering why in the world I was in the ditch. Or I could spend my time gathering my papers to get them back in the basket--so I could go on down the road.

Further, I would later realize that there would be many times I would find someone else in the ditch. I would have two choices then as well. I could keep going and maybe even laugh at the person for being in the ditch, or I could stop and help my neighbor gather his papers so he could get on down the road.

By the way, I never saw Eulan Brown complaining that he was in the ditch. Never did he do that. He was just always gathering the papers and putting them back in his basket so he could go on down the road.

And he absolutely refused to give up.

Eulan Brown chose to live one day at a time. He lived in the moment. He did not spend his energy worrying about what happened yesterday or what caused his plight in life. And he surely didn't concern himself with what would or could happen tomorrow. He just squeezed all he could out of each day.

But Eulan had to know every morning when he left the house to deliver his papers that there would be a good possibility that he would wreck that bicycle and find himself in the ditch. It happened almost every day of his life. But that possibility never stopped him from delivering those papers.And the possibility of failure should never stop us from doing whatever it is we have been called to do.

When I was in high school I played basketball. In the fall of 1970, I was entering my junior year when the public schools were integrated. For me that meant all the great athletes (and basketball players) from Hunt High School in Fort Valley, Ga. were about to converge on Fort Valley High School. The new much larger high school would be called Peach County High School. Not only would it be much more difficult to make the basketball team, but Peach County would also move into the largest classification in the Georgia High School Association. That meant the competition would be much greater than anything I had ever experienced – if I made the team.

The summer before my junior year in high school I made a decision to do everything in my power to prepare myself for the upcoming basketball season. I shot a thousand times a day. I even kept a chart. My dad would let one of the guys who worked at our grocery store come with me to the gym every afternoon after we got off work to throw balls back to me. I shot basketballs until I got blisters on my hand.

When I showed up at the first basketball practice at the new school, I could shoot the lights out of a basketball. I did make the team and actually led that team in scoring for the next two years. I couldn't jump very high and was not fast, but I could shoot.

And I noticed something.

When the game was on the line and we were one point behind with three seconds left on the clock and the coach called time out, most people didn't want the ball. They wanted to be on the winning team, but they didn't want the ball when the game was on the line. I remember always telling the coach to get the ball to me. Give me the ball. But most people in that huddle didn't want to take that last shot because they did not want to risk being the goat. They never experienced making the winning shot, because they were afraid they would miss it and be the goat.

I'll just say it.

You will never become a winner until you get to the point that you are not afraid to lose. You just have to be willing to fail if you want to become a winner. And if you are a winner, you will lose many times along the way.

You can count on that.

I missed more of those shots than I made. But I also made a few. And the shots I made took me to greater levels than those who were afraid to try. I learned from the misses. I would just gather my papers, put them back in the basket and go on down the road. And I became better for it all.

But make no mistake. I was prepared to take that last shot. I didn't come out of the stands and tell the coach to give me the ball on the last play of the game. I shot a thousand times a day, and I had envisioned myself many times being in that situation. I had worked extremely hard to put myself in that situation. And I would even dare to say I had worked harder than anyone else on that team.

So there is another lesson.

In order to be a winner, you have to be willing to get up earlier, leave later, work harder and give everything you've got and more--even to the point of getting blisters on your hand or even to the point of having skinned knees and elbows from falling off a bicycle. Winning does not come without sacrifice.

When Jesus gave that great "Sermon on the Mount," he made some very interesting comments that have always stuck with me. He said, "Enter through the narrow gate. For wide is the gate and broad is the road that leads to destruction, and many enter it. But small is the gate and narrow is the road that leads to life, and only a few find it." *Matthew 7:13-14 NIV*

I won't try to explain what I think about the spiritual message in those verses. I'll let someone else do that. But there is a great principle there.

Most people are walking down the broad road. They get up in the morning with a mindset that says, "What have I got to do to get by today? What have I got to do to keep from losing my job or what have I got to do to keep from getting thrown off the team or what have I got to do to keep from losing my marriage? What have I got to do to keep from losing?"

That is the wide road.

But there are a few people walking down the narrow road. They get up in the morning with the mindset that says what can I do to be the best at what I've been asked to do? What can I do to be better than everyone else?

Just for the record, the wide road leads to mediocrity. The narrow road leads to excellence. And most people live mediocre lives. Only a few people pursue excellence.

By the way, Eulan also taught me that you sure can learn a lot from other folks if you just take the time to know them or live with intent to find them. In my view, God puts people in our path for a reason. Sometimes those people can be "up front and on a stage," sometimes they can be acquaintances we just never take time to really know and sometimes they can be people you would never expect would be there to impact your life.

Eulan Brown, the *Grit* newspaper boy who could not keep his balance, never complained about being in the ditch. When he found himself in the ditch, he spent his energy gathering the papers, so he could get them back in the basket and get on down the road. He was simply not afraid to lose. And giving up was not even in his vocabulary. He kept riding that old bicycle and delivering those newspapers. He worked harder than anyone else because it took so much for him to do what he did every day.

There is no doubt Eulan Brown was one of those few people who walked down the narrow road. And although he had limited abilities and limited resources, he did not live a mediocre life. He made a choice to pursue life. And he absolutely refused to give up in that pursuit.

Introduction

The stories you are about to read were written over a span of three years from 2006 to 2009. Most were written in airports, on airplanes and in hotel rooms late at night or early in the morning. My writing was a way for me to escape from the everyday pressures of business management.

You will quickly discover that there is nothing special about my ability to write.

But there is something special about the people I have written about and the thoughts I have attempted to put on paper. I hope you are just as inspired reading the stories as I have been encouraged by writing them.

I have lived a charmed life. No doubt about it. It sure hasn't been perfect. There have plenty of bumps along the way, and I know there will be more. But it has been charmed because of where I grew up and the people around me who influenced me in such a positive way.

With the exception of my four years at the University of Georgia, I was fortunate and blessed to live in Reynolds, Ga. the first 48 years of my life. I sold my funeral businesses in 1997 and began working in the funeral industry for corporate America. My life changed rapidly as my new job required me to travel extensively. I eventually moved my family about 35 miles away to Warner Robins, Ga.

As a result, my life was again charmed because of other folks I have had the opportunity to know and meet along the way all across our country.

I think you will notice as you read that I am a rather inquisitive person. I got that honestly from my dad. He was always "peeling back the onion" to see the underlying attributes about people and moments that others might have missed.

That is exactly what I have attempted to do here.

The stories I have written are not unlike Eulan Brown's *Grit* newspapers. They have been strewn all over the place. This book is my effort to take some of the stories and get them back in a basket so maybe others can use them and be inspired as they continue down the road of life.

Actually the stories have been placed into four baskets, and the baskets represent four of the major lessons I gleaned from the life of Eulan Brown.

The first basket consists of stories about people who, for various reasons, found themselves in the ditch of life. You will be inspired by the stories of young widows who lost their husbands when they were much too young to lose a husband but somehow put their papers back in the basket and moved on down the road. You will find the story about my lifelong friend whose twin brother saved his life and ended up losing his own. You will be introduced to a girl who survived an automobile crash in which three of her close friends were killed. There is a story about a friend who was dying of cancer and didn't think her life counted for much. There is the story of the famous basketball coach who found himself in the ditch and motivated millions to never give up. You will read about a young lady who lost her job but kept her faith and about a young couple who desperately wanted a child but thought they were destined to never have one. You will get to know a man who has been visiting his wife's grave daily for 27 years, and a man in the prime of his life diagnosed with Lou Gehrig disease. There is a story about my friend who lost all her baggage at an airport. You will get a lesson in pain from a broken toe, and a lesson in relativity when my wife was facing surgery.

The second basket contains stories about the joy and power of living life in the moment. As a lifelong undertaker, I am convinced most people spend way too much time fretting over what happened yesterday or worrying about what may happen tomorrow, and they end up missing the moment they never get back. If anybody ever lived in the moment it was Eulan Brown. So when I meet people who are pursing life in the moment with every fiber of their being or when I experience or even remember the richness special moments in life can bring, I become inspired. In this basket, you will read such varied stories from some college students skipping class to lessons from the game of golf to a special weekend in the mountains to a weekend trip to New York City with a lifelong friend. Hopefully you will be touched by a story from a grandpa when his first grandchild was born. And maybe you will even chuckle a time or two when you read the story of a golf dog.

The third basket is about a few folks I have met along the way who decided somewhere in life they would leave mediocrity behind and pursue excellence. They left the wide road and chose to walk the narrow road to do whatever it takes to make a difference and were not afraid to sacrifice to do it. Some of their stories are finished and some are just beginning. And some will be passed down to other generations. You will be introduced to a grocery store clerk, a corporate executive, a schoolteacher and a young business entrepreneur. There are stories about a humble domestic worker, a young missionary couple and a group of little league coaches. You will read about a women's championship high school basketball team, their coach and mentor and a little league baseball team that defied the odds and won the world championship and showed class while doing it. You will be inspired by the story of a small town doctor, a young man about to be a doctor and a small town athletic hero. There is the story of a house builder who would not lower his standards and a young athlete from a small high school who never gave up and won a scholarship at a major college. And there are the stories of a couple of exceptional girls who happen to be sisters whose stories have just begun. Just like Eulan, these people have inspired me to run from mediocrity. And I think they will inspire you as well.

The last basket contains a collection of writings about people you might miss in life if you don't pay careful attention – just like you might have missed Eulan Brown. It is amazing to me what you can learn about folks if you ask a few questions and choose to look beyond the external layers. You will read about a man everybody knew as "sunshine" and a cab driver in Chicago who just wanted someone to listen. There is a story about a trapper his friends will never forget and a shoeshine man in the airport in Atlanta. There is a story about an old gentleman who seemed not to have a purpose in life and another man who spent his entire life in a mental institution. You will also read about a couple of unassuming farmers who were not only experts in growing food but were also experts in growing families. You will read about a controversial preacher who was not really controversial at all and a railroad depot manager who had a heart of gold. You will read about my friend who was transplanted from New York to Georgia and began sprouting southern roots and another man whose southern roots grow as deep as the Georgia clay.

Although I have written these stories, they are not mine and I claim no ownership.

They are stories, however, of real life and real people as seen through the lenses of a small town fourth generation undertaker from Reynolds.

Basket One

Ditches

"I would later realize that there would be many times in my own life that I would find myself in the ditch with my papers strewn all over the place. I would have two choices. I could spend my time moaning, groaning, complaining and wondering why in the world I was in the ditch. Or I could spend my time gathering my papers to get them back in the basket so I could go on down the road.

I also would later realize that there would be many times I would find someone else in the ditch. I would have two choices then as well. I could keep going and maybe even laugh at the person for being in the ditch or I could stop and help my neighbor gather his papers so he could get on down the road."

Three Things to Do Every Day

I became a Jimmy Valvano fan in 1983 when North Carolina State beat heavily-favored Houston on a last second dunk shot to win the college basketball national championship. I still have the mental picture of Coach Valvano running on the basketball court looking for somebody to hug. It was one of the greatest moments in sports.

I became a bigger fan some 10 years later when I saw him give one of the most powerful speeches I had ever heard in my life. Jimmy V was the recipient of the "Arthur Ashe Courage Award" at the ESPY's in 1993 as he was also dying of cancer. That night he announced the establishment of the Jimmy V Foundation for Cancer Research. Jimmy Valvano died less than two months after giving that speech.

I got home late tonight and was working on some stuff for work and watching ESPN out of the corner of my eye. I starting watching with both eyes when I realized that powerful speech I first heard over 13 years ago was being replayed on television

What he said in that speech has been my philosophy in life. It is certainly what I attempt to do every time I stand in front of an audience to give a speech. But more importantly, it is what I try to do every single day of my life. Sometimes it doesn't work out that way but when it does, I know I've had a great day.

Valvano said this, and I quote, *"To me, there are three things we all should do every day. We should do this every day of our lives. Number one is laugh. You should laugh every day. Number two is think. You should spend some time in thought. And number three is, you should have your emotions moved to tears, could be happiness or joy. But think about it. If you laugh, you think, and you cry, that's a full day. That's a heck of a day. You do that seven days a week, you're going to have something special."*

I love to laugh, and I look for things to make me laugh and love to hang out with people who laugh a lot. I believe it is even okay to laugh in the face of adversity. I have noticed that people don't laugh enough. Some people just take themselves way too seriously. I cut up more than most people. I understand that. But it's important to me. It's who I am. Anybody that has hung around me for any period of time knows that laughter is a major part of who I am.

My responsibility at work is enormous, and I have to think strategically for opportunities and I have to think through problems and the possible solutions to the problems we may face. I get paid to think. And there are huge financial ramifications if I don't think correctly. But I also like to think about the important things of life. I believe the Bible is the greatest book ever written, and it is full of principles for common sense living. I've spent many hours studying it and even memorizing chunks of it. The best thinking I do is when I am attempting to apply those principles to the normal situations of life.

I really don't like to cry, but the older I get the more I do it. You won't find me crying out loud, but it doesn't take much for my eyes to fill up with tears. I was talking to a close friend just today and my eyes filled up with tears because of something very kind she said. My eyes fill up when I look at my daughter-in-law carrying my first grandchild. My eyes filled up with tears yesterday at the thought of an amazing act of kindness by my oldest son eight years ago. Sometimes I cry when I watch others go through their storms. They say men are not supposed to cry. This one does, and I'm not ashamed of it.

It is easy to get these three things out of balance. If we laugh all the time and never think or get emotional we would be a nut case. If we think all the time and never laugh or cry, we would be considered a nerd. If we cry all the time and never laugh or think, we would be admitted to a certain kind of hospital.

It's the balance that is important. When I first started traveling around entertaining people, all I did was the funny stuff. Later, I added a little to my talk to cause people to think and maybe even stretched them to think about things they were not comfortable thinking about. And when I began to let myself be transparent enough to move people emotionally, my speaking career and opportunities to do it really took off.

Here is some absolutely free advice. If you want to really take off in life, make sure you laugh every day of your life and make sure you take the time to think every day of your life. And do not be afraid to cry.

And don't give up. Don't ever ever give up!

I agree with Jimmy Valvano. If you laugh, think and cry seven days a week you're going to have something special. And giving up will not even be in your vocabulary.

December 05, 2006

A Choice We Make

He did everything for her. He made her laugh, made a living and made sure the whole family was in church every time the doors opened. He even did the grocery shopping. One minute he was here. The next minute he was gone. Not just gone on a business trip.

But really gone.

Ralph Rudolph Underwood, age 49, died on May 9, 1972, leaving a young wife and four children to fend for themselves. Irene Underwood became a widow at the young age of 43. Her children were ages 22, 17, 14, and 7. Not a good time for a daddy, role model and provider to go on such an extended trip. But he did anyway.

Life can be like that.

Being in the funeral business, I have seen that scenario play out over and over in the lives of countless numbers of families. The same question continues to be asked. Why?

I have heard plenty of people try to answer that, but to be truthful, I've never heard a good answer.

But, you can learn life lessons from people like Irene Underwood.

Irene did not have a physical handicap like Eulan Brown but she was certainly handicapped – being alone with four children to rear. And there is no doubt she found herself many times in the ditch with her papers strewn everywhere. And I'm sure she must have asked why - more than a few times along the way.

But she always picked up the papers, got back on her bicycle and continued on down the road. The word "quit" was not in her vocabulary--Nor should it be in ours.

I buried Eulan Brown many years ago but I never forgot him. Irene Underwood is my mother-in-law and I will never forget her either.

She finished raising those four children, and they all turned out just fine. They never missed a meal along the way. The word quit is not in their vocabulary either. They carry the lesson their mom taught them everywhere they go.

I've been thinking. Maybe we are asking the wrong question. Maybe the question should not be "why" when we find ourselves in the ditch.

Maybe we should be asking, "How fast we will be able to get our papers back in the basket, get out of the ditch, and get back on our bicycle?"

It is definitely a choice we make.

July 17, 2006

For Everything There is a Season

My mother-in-law has lived with us for the past 4 years or so. She has had a few extended visits with her other children but for the most part she has been a member of our family. She goes wherever we go. She attends church every Sunday with us and goes with us when we go out to eat. I have told all the mother-in-law jokes and I laugh and others laugh and she laughs. I have asked more than a few people if they would like to keep her for a while – that I can have her at their house by 10 a.m. the next day on Federal Express. We laugh and we go on. But tonight I am not laughing.

My mother-in-law is spending her first night in an Assisted Living facility in Warner Robins. I just spoke to my wife on the phone and she is struggling. I could hear it in her voice. She is not struggling about the decision that has been made but she is struggling with the fact her mom is at the place in life where she can no longer be alone. And that is a major event in the life of any child. And it is a major event in the life of any person who has reached that stage in life.

And it is also a major event in the life of a husband who cannot be there for his wife on this "major event" night. But thankfully her sisters are there with her and that is probably exactly the way it should be. God has a way of working those things out.

Thankfully my mother-in-law is excited about her new apartment and her move. She and her children actually visited the facility with the prospect of her staying at this facility only during the day while Kathy was at school. But when she visited and saw it, she immediately decided she wanted to move in. A woman of great faith, she said that moving to this facility is the next step toward heaven. I don't know how anyone could have a better attitude. My wife and her sisters have spent the weekend decorating her room to make it just right. And I can tell you it is just right.

Truthfully her time at our house the last four years has not come without sacrifice. Anybody who has ever had a parent live in your home knows what I am talking about. My wife has had a few meltdowns. And I have had a few meltdowns. I'll never forget the time I came home late one night from traveling to find my mother-in-law in my bed under the covers on my side, sound asleep. And there have been a few times I wanted to take a shower, and my mother-in-law was in it. And there have been a few Saturdays I wanted to take a nap on the sofa, and the sofa was taken. And there were a few times my wife and I needed to have a private conversation that we could not have. And there have been a few times we were late to church or didn't get to go to church. And there were times I would have much rather eaten dinner alone with my wife. And the restaurant checks have been higher more than a few times because we had an extra person on the bill. And I could go on.

But it is not what we take up, but what we give up that makes us rich.

And in giving up some things, we gained so much more than we would have gained if we chose not to give it up. There is no doubt that one of these days we will look back on these past four years and realize they were the richest years of our lives. I saw a daughter get to spend a lot of time with her mother who sacrificed much more for her own kids than we ever sacrificed for her. And I saw my own children get to spend an awful lot of quality time with the only grandparent they have living. And memories have been created that will be passed down for generations to come. And this son-in-law had some long conversations with an exceptional human being who did an amazing job as a single parent under very difficult circumstances. And I learned a lot about her and a lot about life.

To receive the level of care she deserves and has earned, the time has come for my mother-in-law to move to this facility. There is no doubt this move is the right thing to do. But she will have more visits that she can imagine. When I drive into town from who knows where, I have a strong feeling my first stop before I get home will always be to check on her. I can make her laugh. And you can bet your bottom dollar I will keep on making her laugh until there are no more smiles in her. Years ago my mother-in-law owned a flower shop. She had these words from Ecclesiastes painted on the door of that shop: "For everything there is a season."

That is really true. And we are living it out right now.

August 06, 2007

Nothing is Impossible with God

When I grew up, Sunday church lasted no more than an hour and Sunday school was about 45 minutes. They had a few people show up for Sunday night services and less than that for the Wednesday night service. Each sermon consisted of three points and a poem. Some could deliver those points better than others and those ministers had bigger churches than the ones who were less talented.

Things are changing in the church world.

A few weeks ago we visited Andy Stanley's North Point Community Church in Atlanta with our son and his wife. They have a different method of doing church, and what they are doing is working. The church we attend in Warner Robins is on the leading edge of using different methods to reach people. And that strategy is also working.

Michael Catt, the Senior Pastor of Sherwood Baptist Church in Albany, Ga., believes his church can reach the world from that South Georgia town.

I happen to believe him.

We went to see the movie, "FACING THE GIANTS" last night. The movie was produced by Sherwood Pictures, Sherwood Baptist's unique film-making ministry. The cast of the movie was made up of local volunteers. Alex Kendrick and Stephen Kendrick are associate pastors at Sherwood Baptist. These two, along with their brother Shannon, wrote and produced the movie. Alex played the lead part of the head football coach. The coach's wife in the movie was played by the real life coach's wife at Sherwood Academy in Albany. And the list goes on.

It took six weeks to film this movie with a two week break in the middle. Incredibly the movie was shot with one high-definition camera and edited on a PowerMac–G-5 computer using some purchased software. Sherwood Pictures rented video and film equipment and work trucks.

Sherwood approached Provident Music Group in Nashville for permission to use songs by Provident artists *Third Day* and *Casting Crowns.* Provident's president viewed the film, liked what he saw and began discussions with Sherwood to oversee the film's distribution. Provident Films showed the film to Sony Pictures. Samuel Goldwyn Pictures, through its relationship with Sony, agreed to distribute the film nationally.

Nothing is impossible with God.

I did not know any of those facts about the making of the movie when I went to see it yesterday. My impression at the beginning of the movie was that you could tell the acting was not professional. I was wondering where they got these actors to play these parts.

I don't know if the acting got better or what, but within 30 minutes I didn't think about the acting again. I was caught up in the story of the movie and more importantly the message of the movie. I can tell you I cried more at this movie than I did when Old Yeller died in his movie.

Afterwards, I left this movie motivated with a stronger desire to face my giants and a stronger desire to help others face theirs. When I saw "Old Yeller," I just wanted to go pat my dog.

The underlying message of the movie is that we all face giants in our lives. And no matter how big the giant and how impossible the situation looks, nothing is impossible with God.

Critics will say (and have said) the movie is unrealistic, because it represents that if you have faith in God, all your problems will work out to your satisfaction.

Those critics miss the point. The message is simply that our faith can be exercised in all facets of our life and nothing is impossible with God.

Just a suggestion from a country undertaker…

If you are facing giants in your life and you really don't see the light at the end of the tunnel, take the time to watch this movie.

Oh . . . be sure to have some tissues with you. You will need them.

But be prepared to leave with a new perspective on life.

December 28, 2006

Making Her Mark

This letter showed up in my mailbox:

Bruce,

I've read your book, "View From a Hearse," and I've read other articles you have written. It never ceases to amaze me at some of the things you come up with, the way you convey them to your readers and the memories you always seem to bring to my mind with your stories. You have such a gift. I know you've been told this many, many times, but I KNOW you do.

I remember going into the grocery store as I was growing up and seeing your dad there. Aunt Ruth would always give me a nickel to get a candy bar or pack of gum or something and tell me how she sure wished my mama and daddy could get my teeth fixed (I know she meant no harm but I was already self-conscious enough about my teeth). I don't know if your daddy heard her or not but he would always say something to make me smile and then tell me I was just about the prettiest thing he'd ever seen. He made me forget about my crooked teeth. Moreover, he made me feel special; like I was somebody, just for him speaking to me.

I can't recall a time ever seeing you out somewhere that you didn't know who I was and speak to me in the same way your daddy did--just as you did Saturday night. It was good to see you at the reunion. Everyone had a wonderful time. I know I did.

I read your stories about your granddaughter, and I have to tell you I have two now; one is four, the other was just born January 14 of this year. The first one took me in tailspin. My family all used to talk about the fact that my children were always my world, my whole life. I didn't think I could love a grandchild any more, and I don't guess I do really but it's different. Sally Kate wrapped me around her little finger from the very first moment after I saw her come into this world. She loves her "gamma" and she knows her gamma loves her. My daughter allowed me the privilege of witnessing the miracle of birth once again when Leah graced our lives in January. I have to say it was the most awesome thing I've ever had the privilege to be a part of. There's nothing like grandchildren! God has blessed us with two of the most beautiful little girls that He possibly could. I understand perfectly the message you were trying to convey in your stories about your granddaughter, Taylor. I know I don't have to tell you this, but spend every moment you can with her. Love her. Know her, and let her know you. Let her learn what an awesome grandpa she has in that he has served God, his family and his friends all his life.

I have pancreatic cancer, diagnosed about a year and a half ago. Although I have already lived much, much longer than any of the doctors in Macon, Emory and Texas said I would, I know my days are numbered. I keep fighting, and I keep telling myself I'm going to beat it. Every day when I wake up, I thank God for letting me have another day with my family, especially my granddaughters. You have a unique opportunity for your granddaughter to know you. Don't waste it.

You have done so well with your life. I know your mama and daddy are so proud of you. You are leaving your mark on the world with your stories. You're touching so many lives. I have not left a mark and now it's too late. Unfortunately, my granddaughters are so young that they will only know me through pictures in the family album and what their mama tells them about me.

Keep up your good work and take care. May God continue to bathe you in His love and care.

Lisa Nelson Windham

Lisa gave me permission to use this personal letter. Lisa passed away on March 30, 2008 after a gallant fight with pancreatic cancer. As a memorial to Lisa who thought she had not left her mark on the world, I thought it important to let her elegant words and wisdom be included here. May the words and the memory of my friend Lisa mark your life.

April 5, 2008

Bad Day

There was a song that was made very popular last year on the hit TV show "American Idol." I'm sure you remember the words:

"You had a bad day. You're taking one down. You sing a sad song just to turn it around. You say you don't know. You tell me don't lie. You work at a smile and you go for a ride. You had a bad day."

My friends, Reginald and Anita Smith of Macon, Ga. had a bad day this past Sunday. They are working at a smile, and I'm not sure they went for a ride. But it was a bad day.

And it is not exactly over.

This happily married couple who have been married around 40 years had been out of town for the weekend. When they arrived back home on Sunday afternoon, Reg opened his mail and noticed a letter to him from a law firm from a town about 100 miles south of Macon. As you could imagine, a personal letter from an unfamiliar attorney got his attention.

When Reg, who happens to be a well known businessman in town, read the letter he almost fainted. He immediately read the letter to his wife. The letter from the attorney stated that a young girl from another town had a baby in January, and she had named him as a potential father. Reg was ordered to come to this town for DNA tests.

You think I'm kidding?

Not only had my friend not been to that town in years where this alleged roll in the onion field happened, but he also had a vasectomy about 30 years ago.

After the shock of the letter, they laughed and called their daughter who lives in another state. She laughed with them and told her dad he needed to keep it in his pants. My friend laughingly said he has had many conversations with his daughter over the years but never had she told him that.

The next day he called the attorney's office and finally had a clerk call him back. He explained to her they obviously had the wrong person. Her response was that she had worked at the law firm for many years, and they had never made the mistake of sending such a letter to the wrong person.

He assured her they had this time.

The crazy thing is that he still is not sure if he has been excused from having to show up for DNA tests in this unnamed town.

The thought of my 60 year old friend driving 100 miles and arriving at Family and Children Services in his black business suit and having to stand in line to get his DNA test done to see if he is the father of this baby makes me laugh. Out loud.

I would pay money to be in the waiting room to watch my friend waiting in line with the other potential dads to get checked. I would love to have a picture of that.

The camera doesn't lie. You're coming back down and you really don't mind. You had a bad day.

Yep, that my friend, is a bad day.

April 11, 2007

The Price of Parenthood

(Birmingham, Ala.) Last night, since I was in town, I drove out to watch my friend and co-worker's 12 year old son from Oxford, Ala. play baseball. Trey Coile was handpicked to be on a traveling team from Birmingham that is heading for a tournament in Cooperstown, N.Y. in a few weeks. He has been injured and out of commission for several weeks. This was Trey's first game back, and he had a difficult time throwing strikes on the mound last night. It was obvious that this young athlete has not had many moments in his life when he struggled on a baseball field. He usually dominates.

I watched as Trey's parents, Michael and Tracey, struggled with their son from the stands. They never took their eyes off him as he struggled on the mound. They moaned and groaned with each pitch that was not a strike, but they never stopped encouraging him. They were focused on one thing. They wanted their son to succeed. There was no way they could separate themselves from what he was going through. In fact, they probably hurt more than he did. Tracey said her stomach was in knots. Michael was analyzing every pitch. "His release is not right... His back leg is dragging... His delivery is not as smooth as usual . . ." Their eyes were absolutely glued on him. They watched every move. Tracey told her husband to go sit somewhere else. He made her nervous too.

And it was just a baseball game. Not an important baseball game either.

I didn't bother to tell them the experience they had at the ballgame is a shadow of things to come. Trey will have many more successes in life than he will have struggles. You can look at him and know that.

But the struggles will come.

They do for all of us.

The truth is Michael and Tracey will never be able to separate themselves from whatever struggles Trey may face. When the struggles come, and they will, their stomach will be in knots and they will try to analyze every move and they will probably make each other nervous. There may be even a few sleepless nights along the way. The stakes will get higher too.

It is the price of parenthood. We pay it when they are kids, and we pay it when they grow up. I have a strong feeling we pay that price until the day we die.

But the dividends we reap sure are worth much more than the price we pay.

By the way you might want to write Trey Coile's name down somewhere. I have a feeling you will be reading about him in the sports pages in a few years.

July 13, 2006

We Really Do Need Each Other

My friend, David Gligor, is on crutches today with a broken leg and has been recuperating from a broken shoulder, broken collarbone, broken ribs and a punctured lung. He is very much aware that he is very fortunate to be alive. The first time I met David was when he became my boss, and to be honest, I had some apprehension about the prospects of him being my boss. I could not help but wonder how a young up and comer corporate guy who grew up in Ohio would mesh with a gray haired southern drawl talking guy from Georgia. When I found out he was of the Orthodox Greek faith, I also wondered how my Southern Baptist and United Methodist background would fit.

To keep you from being in suspense, I will go ahead and answer that question. It was a perfect fit. Just so you will know I am not trying to get brownie points with my boss, David is no longer my boss. After working for him for 3 years or so, David transferred to another area of responsibility, and I was fortunate enough to take his position. So for the past couple of years, we have been peers.

When I began working for David, I quickly realized I had never met a man who worked harder. He was absolutely wide open. Most nights we would get to a hotel after midnight, and we would leave again at 6 a.m. I also quickly realized that he was very smart, and I had sense enough to make it my business to learn all I could from him. He was a very tough businessman and did not hesitate to make the tough decisions. He took me to a completely different level in my profession, and he made me very tired trying to keep up with him.

But I think I helped him out a little as well. David did not have a funeral background, and since I have been in the business since before I was old enough to drive, I was able to help him understand the importance of our people who sit across the desk from families who have had their hearts ripped out day after day. Further, I know what it takes to look after all the intricate and very important details from the time a death call is received until the disposition takes place.

We realized we were in a very good situation. We learned from each other and we both had great respect for each other. Since we spent so much time together traveling throughout the United States, we talked about everything under the sun. We had many serious discussions about life, but we also laughed a lot. It didn't take me long to realize that this very tough businessman had a huge heart. During our time of working together his very beautiful and young wife found out she had cancer. In what seemed like a blink of an eye she was gone and David's world was rocked. I visited Debbie at a Houston hospital just a couple of days before she passed away. It was a moment, and a visit I will never forget. In just a few days I was serving as a pallbearer at her funeral. I watched my completely devastated friend trying to get his breath. At the same time I saw a very smart tough businessman go to a completely different level in understanding what our profession is all about.

David made it through the darkest days of his life as everybody eventually does. He was very determined to keep living life to the fullest. He is now recuperating because he was racing his dirt bike a few months ago one Saturday afternoon and took a major spill. It is a miracle he made it out alive.

A few months ago, David paid me the greatest compliment he could possibly pay me. He told me that when his future son-in-law asked for his daughter's hand in marriage, he had one request before he agreed. He wanted his future son-in-law to watch a video of one of my talks.

The relationship I have with David Gligor taught me a very valuable lesson. It doesn't matter where we come from or what our background happens to be, there really are no differences. We all need to continually work to build relationships with those God puts in our path. Those relationships can be the catalyst to help us live out what we were put on earth to do. We make each other better.

We really do need each other

June 27, 2007

He Told Her He Would

On March 20, 1959, Corine Johnson visited my dad for the purpose of paying for her funeral expenses in advance. Fearing she didn't have much time to live and fearing that her son, Ephraim, didn't have much time either, she also paid for Ephraim's funeral at the same time. Ephraim had been sickly and in the mental hospital in Milledgeville for 13 years when his mom paid for his funeral expenses in 1959. He was admitted to Central State Hospital when he was 24 years old.

She casually asked daddy that day if he would be willing to look after Ephraim in case her son outlived her. There was no other family.

Daddy told her he would.

Corine's funeral bill was $575.79. Ephraim's was three dollars less. Corine's bill included a burial dress for $23. Eprhaim's bill did not include a burial dress but did include a trip to Milledgeville to pick him up and bring him back to Reynolds at his death. The charge for that was $3 less than the dress.

Corine died four years later. Ephraim is still living in Milledgeville. He didn't pass away as quickly as his mom thought he would. And the interest is still growing on the $20 she paid to bring him back to Reynolds.

Daddy found that Corine had been serious about asking him to look after her son. He was named in her will as the person to look after Ephraim. She had been very serious.

I'm not sure about the status the first four years after Corine's death, but in 1963 Daddy was appointed legal guardian for Ephraim K. Johnson, and he served in that capacity for 31 years until the day he died.

I remember every Christmas daddy would have the ladies who worked at his store make a Christmas package for Ephraim, and they would ship it to Milledgeville. He made sure he had funds in his personal account in Milledgeville. For many years, the state took care of the tab for people like Ephraim and daddy managed and invested Ephraim's money, which consisted of the accumulation of a monthly social security check. Several years before daddy died the state changed that policy and Ephraim had to start paying his way until the funds were depleted.

A few months before daddy died, I drove him to Milledgeville to visit with Ephraim. I found out that day from the staff at Central State that he has not spoken one word since the day he was admitted in that hospital. At that visit it had been 48 years since he became a patient at Central State. And it had been 48 years since he had spoken a word.

It has been 60 years now. Can you imagine being a patient in a hospital for 60 years? And not speaking a word to anyone?

The day we visited Ephraim in that hospital, daddy knew he (daddy) probably didn't have long to live. He asked me on the way home that day if I would take over the guardianship at his death.

He had made a promise to a widow woman 34 years earlier.

I said I would.

And I did. And I still do.

For the past 12 years I have been the legal guardian for Ephraim Johnson. The only time I ever saw him was that day I took daddy over to visit.

Every month he receives a check from Social Security and every month I write a check to Central State Hospital on his behalf to pay for his stay. Every month or two I get a call or a letter from his caseworker giving me an update on his health or getting permission to do a procedure at the doctor's office. Once a year I have to complete a host of forms to prove that Ephraim is still eligible for Medicaid.

I completed those forms tonight.

For a man that owns nothing and has spent the last 60 years quietly in an institution, it is not hard to prove.

When I think things are going bad for me and such things happen as getting stuck in a traffic jam or having a delayed flight or not getting what I want for supper or not getting to see my favorite TV show or seeing my favorite team lose the game....

I need to think of Ephraim K. Johnson.

I don't have it nearly as bad as I think.

Neither do you if you are able to read this.

Corine had no idea when she made her *Last Will and Testament* that 43 years later her son would still be living. I would imagine she prayed that he wouldn't be. I don't know why God would keep a person like that in that kind of shape around so long.

But somehow I would imagine He is trying to teach the rest of us some important things about living life.

Oct 4, 2006

Leon and Mandy Made a Commitment

My wife's dad died suddenly when she was a junior in high school. He was only 49 years old. That seems really young to me these days. His wife, who is now my mother-in-law, became a widow at age 43. That also seems really young to me.

As you can imagine, those were some tough days for a 43 year old mother left with four children ranging in age from 7 to 22. It was tough on the mother, and it was tough on those four children. As most people do, this family somehow survived the heartache and pain and hopelessness that death has a way of delivering to loved ones left behind.

I think there are several reasons this family made it through this heart wrenching experience. The most important was their faith. The fact that this family depended on their faith when things were going well sure did help when the rug was pulled out from under them. They were able to believe what they could not see. They also had many friends who rallied around them. Again, the fact that this family was friendly to people when things were going well sure did help when the rug was pulled out from under them. True friends have a way of showing up in the middle of the greatest storms of life.

They also had a large supportive family. I am not sure how this story would have turned out (or stories like this would turn out) if not for family. In my line of work, I have seen it so many times. Close families depend on each other in a way they never dreamed when invaded by death. Families that are not close will tend to be torn apart permanently during the trials of life. This was a close family.

Leon Windham was one of this young widow's brothers. He and his wife Mandy made a decision to be there for them. It was more that a decision actually. It was a commitment.

For several Christmases after Ralph Underwood's death, Leon and Mandy brought their two young children to the Underwood's house for Christmas. They knew the Christmas season would be a very difficult time for this family, so they decided to do something about it. The doing something about it had to take some major sacrificing on their part. They showed up year after year with two small children and their Santa Claus to celebrate with this family who had their collective heart ripped out.

They brought with them gifts for all and so many laughs and so much fun. And when my wife's family looks back, they realize those days were some of the richest days of their lives.

The Windhams challenged a very tough situation, and with purpose and a lot of passion, Leon and Mandy turned it into something really good.

Why am I writing about this tonight? My wife and I were talking a few days ago about the impact Leon and Mandy had on their lives when they desperately needed impacting. Funny thing the next day their daughter, Jill, emailed me with a picture of them attached.

And there is a lesson for all of us in this story.

God puts people in our lives for a reason. Make no mistake about that. There are times when a phone call or a visit or a card is exactly what is needed. But sometimes the need is much more. To meet that need takes some serious investment in the lives of the people God has put in our lives.

Leon and Mandy did some serious investing, and they made a huge difference in the life of this family. I saw it first hand and experienced it. And tonight 35 years later, I have a great appreciation for their investment and am very thankful for their sacrifice. Although they may not realize it, what they did still impacts this family today.

What we do today for others not only impacts them today but can also still be impacting 35 years from now.

I kind of think only in giving of ourselves do we ever find the true meaning of life. Somewhere along the way Leon and Mandy figured that out.

March 28, 2007

Till Death Do Us Part

A co-worker and I drove through a cemetery today and saw a gentleman trimming shrubbery at his family plot. We stopped to visit with him.

Although there are plenty of maintenance workers in the cemetery, he insists on taking care of his own landscaping on the property he owns. He told me he has been coming to the cemetery every day since his wife died.

He began to cry. As he was speaking, I looked at the death date on the memorial. I was expecting to see that his wife had died recently.

She died in 1982. That would be 27 years ago.

I also discovered the nice gentleman had the same death date on his memorial. "When she died," he explained, "I died with her." I believed him.

But I had to find out more. He married her when he was 23 and she was 20. She worked while he got his college degree. They moved out west and then later moved back to Louisiana. They started a business that turned out to be a very successful one. She was his business partner and office manager.

She died of cancer in the prime of their marriage when she was 48 years old. Because he couldn't go back to that business without his wife, he sold the thriving business soon after her death and retired at age 53.

He said he visits her grave every day – rain or shine. Sometimes he visits twice a day. That would be more than 10,000 visits in case you are counting.

Most would say his behavior is not healthy, and he should have gone on with his life. And I certainly understand that thinking.

But in a time when married couples are leaving each other on a whim for almost any reason or even no reason at all, I couldn't help but be impressed.

Many years ago this man met the love of his life and told her he loved her. I couldn't help but wonder if she knew just how much he really did love her.

Fifty five years ago he looked at his bride and said, "Till death do us part."

I can tell you he wasn't paying one bit of attention to that statement today.

April 28, 2009

He Always Has a Plan

Chalk one up for the good guys.

Or good gal in this case.

Actually you can chalk one up for a good God who came through just in the nick of time for one beautiful southern belle by the name of Cindy Comperry.

Cindy graduated from the University of Tennessee in 1995 with a communication degree, which made sense to me since her dad is a professional "communicator" in the form of a Methodist minister. Not long after her graduation, Cindy landed a job with the American Cancer Society in Nashville and used her education in a wonderful way as she worked to raised funds for such a worthy cause.

After about nine years of fund raising for the ACS, Cindy changed careers and began working as a promotions director for a communication company. This job was right up her alley, and she found herself traveling to other parts of the country. She was happy as a lark and sailing right on through life with the wind at her back.

Until about six months ago.

Cindy went in to work one winter day and found that her job had been eliminated. She became another victim of the economic train wreck of our good ol' U.S. of A. Not a comfortable position for a young single female who had spent the last fourteen years making her own living.

The good news is Cindy did not panic. She corresponded with her network of friends and business associates looking for good advice. Her Methodist upbringing didn't hurt either because she also spent a great deal of time corresponding with her heavenly network. Her verse for the past six months was from *Hebrews* 11:1 NIV, "Faith is being sure of what we hope for and certain of what we do not see."

Cindy was sure of what she hoped for. And though she will freely admit she worried and wavered a few times about being certain of what she could not see, she kept the faith. And she waited and prayed. And others waited and prayed with her.

Today, Cindy's faith is much stronger than it has ever been. And her faith is stronger than it would have been if she had not gone through six months without a job.

The truth is when Cindy was wavering, God was not. He had a plan all the time and at just the right time He would show up.

Her unemployment checks were scheduled to end next week.

On Friday, Cindy accepted a job doing what she has been training to do for the last 14 years. Talk about timing. Mind you, Cindy did not know she had been in training for this new job... but God did.

Even when it seems the walls are coming down and our world is falling apart, God is always in control.

He always has a plan.

And the Vanderbilt Children's Hospital will now be beneficiaries of His plan.

August 01, 2009

Homes Last Forever

Our phone started ringing early at our house today. Friends from our hometown of Reynolds were letting us know that the house in which we raised our family had burned to the ground. Thankfully, nobody was hurt or killed.

But at least a thousand memories ran through my mind as I drove to my office this morning. And a huge lump was in my throat when I drove over this afternoon to visit my friends who had purchased the house from us and to see what's left of the place where our children grew up.

I was playing golf one afternoon in the fall of 1987 and was driving in a golf cart down number 9 fairway when I saw my friend and realtor, Pete Ayers, putting a For Sale sign in the yard of that house. I finished playing golf that day and went straight home and told my wife that the house we had always wanted was for sale. In a matter of weeks, we sold our house and purchased the beautiful house that sat next to Number 9 fairway.

I can tell you there was a lot of living in that house before we ever bought it. In fact, the Bond family lived there for 38 years. Mr. and Mrs. H.C. Bond and family were there long before we took over. I remember being very proud to be moving in the Bond home, and I think Mrs. Bond was proud as well.

When we moved in, I was only 33 years old and Kathy was 32. Our boys were seven, six and two. When we moved sixteen years later, Kathy and I were both 48 – the boys were 23, 21, and 17. I can tell you we did a lot of living in that house. And a whole lot of learning. There was also a lot of praying when our boys got older and were out and about and doing who knows what. Thankfully the praying paid off. They never got killed or killed anyone else, and they all turned out fine. But I have to admit I did wonder a time or two if they would make it.

About a year after we moved in, we bought a Yellow Lab and named her Abby. She was a part of our family for almost the entire time we were there. To say Abby was known by all the golfers would be a huge understatement. She became an institution at the Reynolds Golf Club.

The house was always full of boys. I remember literally stepping over kids sleeping all over the floor of the den on a weekend when I would leave in the middle of the night to go on a death call. The Johnson girls lived across the golf course, and they came in and out as much as our own boys. And there were the cousins who came on many weekends and spent weeks at a time in the summer…and the Harrell cousins who visited their grandparents next door.

My goodness there was a lot of living in that house.

For some of you golfers who are reading this who thought you were stung by a wasp when you bent over to tee up your ball, I have come to find out later in life it wasn't a wasp. You probably were shot by a BB gun by one of my boys with their cousins and/or friends dressed in camouflage hiding in the bushes.

Later the girlfriends came. And my goodness they were cute, and I had so much fun. I was sitting in the den one night listening to one of my sons break up with his very cute girlfriend. I almost fainted when he told her he felt like he needed to spend more time with his truck.

There were times in the later years when we would have girl spend the night parties. And I would step over girls when I left the house in the middle of the night.

I thought today of the time that I drove up and thought there had been a murder. There was blood all under the carport and on the brick walls. My heart dropped to my stomach. I remember being relieved when I discovered that John and his friend Syd had picked up a possum on the highway and skinned it under our carport.

I also remember driving up one afternoon and seeing my mother fall as she was walking in the side door. I got her up off the floor and took her to her doctor in Macon that day. He admitted her and she died less than a week later. I also remember my dad eating his last meal in the dining room of that house. I took him back home that night and found him dead the next morning.

When I stood this afternoon looking at the remnants of the place we once called home, I swallowed hard.

But I was reminded of something very important.

Houses can be destroyed overnight.

But homes last forever.

March 13, 2009

He Never Did Really Quit Living

Thirty-five years ago today I was sitting in study hall at Peach County High School. I was a senior and had only a couple of weeks left in my high school career. The main thing I had on my mind was trying to decide if I was going to play college basketball. I had been invited to several schools and had already practiced with several college teams. I had an invitation later in the week to practice with another college in north Georgia. I had already been accepted at the University of Georgia, but I could not decide whether I should go there and forget basketball or go to a smaller college and play.

The day before, my girlfriend and I visited her dad who was a patient at Sams-Whatley hospital in Reynolds. He laughed and cut up as he normally did, and we talked about my future basketball career. He also laughingly warned me to take care of his daughter. I had been dating her a year by then so I knew her dad well. I was a little afraid of him, but he was always joking and picking at me.

The Underwoods drove a white station wagon and many times the whole family went on excursions together. For the past several months, I had been the driver on those family outings. I had become part of the family. But I was always warned to quit looking at his daughter and keep my eye on the road.

Anyway, the announcement came on the intercom that afternoon in the study hall for me to come to the office. I thought I was in trouble. When I got to the office, the secretary told me to call my mom. I did that and almost lost my breath when she told me that Ralph Underwood had passed away. How could that be? I just saw him the day before. I had never been so shocked in my life. He had just turned 49 years old. That seemed a lot older back then than it does now, but it was way too young.

I left school and drove in a daze straight to my girlfriend's house which was about 20 miles away. When I drove up, there were already a lot of cars in the yard. I walked in the door, and the first person I saw was my girlfriend's mom. She hugged me. She had never hugged me in my life. She was a very strong woman and was not a hugger. I still remember her words: "What are we going to do?"

Thirty-five years later, this is what they did.

After a lot of grief and a lot of help and a lot of faith, somehow they survived. And they kept living. The four children all grew up and had kids of their own. I married my girlfriend a little over five years later. Ralph Underwood now has ten grandchildren and three great grandchildren, but he never got to hold any of them. And none of them ever got to sit in his lap. But all of us who knew him sure can see him in each one of his grandchildren.

So although he is not here physically, he is still very much alive in his children and his grandchildren. When you think about it, a person never does really ever quit living.

That is especially true when he spends his life investing in those people entrusted to him.

He did. And we all remember.

Especially on May 9th.

May 09, 2007

Please Tell Me I'm Right

Yesterday afternoon, I was moving a glass end table (actually a heavy glass end table) out to our storage building. Being the stupid guy I am, I didn't bother to remove the glass from the table before I moved the table. I think I thought the glass was secured.

To make a stupid story even more stupid, it wasn't. And the heavy piece of glass came off the table top and hit me on the big toe.

I got a quick real life lesson in pain.

After a few moments of extreme shock and numbness, I somehow completed the job I had started. I was hoping I could walk off the pain.

I made it back inside to the sofa, and I realized this particular pain was not the walk off variety. I was hurting from the tip of my toe to my ear lobes. There was a basketball game on TV, and I can promise you I didn't know who was winning or who was playing. In an attempt to get relief, I made it into the kitchen and filled a bucket with ice and water to soak my toe.

Later the intense unbearable pain began to subside and I moved into the aching throbbing stage. I eventually was able to make it upstairs and tell my wife what had happened. I could now at least communicate with the world around me.

We went out to eat with friends last night and although I complained about my toe killing me all night, I could now discuss other subjects and carry on normal conversations about things other than my hurting toe.

This morning I woke up to a rough looking toe. I put my shoe on and limped my way to church, determined not to let the aching toe stop me from living. I do wonder how I will make it walking through airports this next week and getting to all the places I have to be, but I will. I will be slower than normal and there will be pain and sometimes severe pain when I step or move in the wrong direction.

Eventually the toe will get back to normal, and I will be back to the point where pain is not the object of my focus.

I tell you all this because some of you can relate. Maybe the pain you experienced is not an aching toe but an aching heart.

At first you were in a state of shock before the piercing pain set in. When the piercing pain began, all you could do was be overwhelmed with the pain. There was nothing else in the world. When you made it through that stage, you were then able to talk about your pain to others and communicate with the world around you. Finally you started doing the normal things of life although you were handicapped and still experienced the pain.

Eventually you got back to the point where the pain was not the object of your focus.

Or for some of us, eventually we will.

Pain is pain regardless of the source. And somehow we get through it and cope and move on with life.

Please tell me I'm right.

January 11, 2009

You Only Have One Mama

Some people are married to more than one person in a lifetime. Most married people have several children and at least a half dozen dogs in a lifetime. Some people are fortunate enough to have several real friends. Most of us have several really important people in our lives.

But you only have one Mama.

Mine was born Naia Gonzalez on July 5, 1917. She was the granddaughter of one of the first Spanish settlers of Fort Myers, Fla.

Her dad, Clyde, died of a heart attack when he was 39 years old. He was sitting on the front porch when it happened. Mama was only thirteen years old, and she was on the porch with him that night. She would tell us later that she screamed and yelled as she ran to the doctor's house down the street for help. The help she sought couldn't help her dad.

That event was a defining moment in her life. She told all her children about that night many times. In our business, she also was able to help many other thirteen year olds in life who had lost a parent.

She understood.

I loved my Mama. She was the best of the best. I know I'm biased but she was something else. She knew how to have fun and she knew how to get serious. She was completely involved in her children's lives. And she was a praying Mom. I mean a down on your knees praying Mom. I'm convinced those Mama's prayers saved my life a few times late at night during my college years.

Understand, she was not perfect, and she never pretended to be. I think that's what made her so great. She was just real.

One of my defining moments came a little over a month from my 39th birthday. Mama was very sick. She had heart problems along with other medical problems. The doctor told us she would not make it. All of her children and spouses and grandchildren surrounded her for several days. The last couple of days we thought every breath would be her last.

She knew she was at the end of her earthly life.

The question that suddenly came out of her mouth could only come from the wife and mother of a bunch of undertakers: *"Is Bruce going to embalm me when I die?"* I was not in the room but the answer was something like I'm sure he will if that is want you want.

She died a couple of days later.

And I did it. I embalmed my Mama. I prepared her body for burial. Talk about defining moments.

I was doing okay in the preparation room until I looked in her eyes. Those were the most familiar eyes I have ever known. It dawned on me that I had first begun to look in those eyes when she rocked me as a baby, and I had never stopped looking into them.

I wept more at that moment than I had all my life added together. It was uncontrollable weeping. I got it all out right there. All the love I felt for my one Mama came out right there from the innermost part of my being.

It was a defining moment in my life. For the first time I think I understood how much I loved my Mama.

And I was able to get a much better understanding of how others loved their Mama when they were in my care at the funeral home.

From that moment on I became much better at what I did for a living.

I also made up my mind that day that though she was dead physically, she would never die in me. If I have had 1,200 speaking engagements to date, I have talked about my Mama 1,200 times.

By the way, she died on August 9, 1993. Exactly thirteen years ago today.

If your mom is still alive, find her today. Look in those familiar eyes if you can. If not, at least give her a call.

And tell her how much you love her.

You only have one Mama.

August 9, 2006

My Cheree Amour

In light of what happened on Wall Street today, maybe this story will remind us that in spite of how dark it seems to get, the sun will come up again.

Although I had known Cheree since she was a little girl, I really got to know her during the darkest day of her life. When you spend your life in the funeral business, it's not difficult to get to know people on the darkest day of their life.

Cheree was only 28 years old on April 22, 1995 when her husband suddenly died of a heart attack. There is no way I can even begin to explain how devastated this young wife was that day, and I cannot even begin to explain how my heart went out to her.

It was like her burden became my burden.

I spent a lot of time with Cheree those days leading up to and following her husband's funeral. We developed a special relationship and bond that will last the rest of our lives. She unknowingly did more for me than I ever did for her.

And I am certain she wondered if she would ever be able to function normally again.

There were many prayers that were prayed on Cheree's behalf for many months following David's death, and I was one of those praying. She was beautiful and sweet and in my opinion she really did not deserve what she had to walk through. "God, please give her life again," I prayed. And I knew in my heart He would.

And oh He did.

"Life again" for her came in the form of the man she would marry some five years later. Cheree and Walker Fricks have been married for eight years now, and they are enjoying life. The rain has turned to sunshine. The darkness has turned to bright day.

Every time I see her we both smile and hug and tell each other how much we love each other. We have a special bond because we walked together years ago down the most difficult path this life can take.

Maybe, we all need to do a little more walking down paths with those who could use a hand to hold or a shoulder to lean on during the dark times. The person who gets leaned on gets as much out of those walks as the person doing the leaning.

Today, I am very thankful I was there, and I am glad she was there.

And I am honored to call Cheree my friend.

September 29, 2008

He Would Be Proud

Kathy and I went to the wedding of the daughter of a longtime friend on Saturday night in the Atlanta area. While there I had the opportunity to visit with the family of another longtime friend. I can tell you a lot of memories flooded my mind as I left that wedding party last night. And I left thinking about how special these folks are to me.

I'll try to explain.

I met Tim Teck my freshman year at University of Georgia. That was 35 years ago in case you are wondering. We had a class together and quickly became friends. We ending up joining the same fraternity and were in the same pledge class. I think, with maybe one exception, we ended up having every class together for the next four years, but somehow we ended up with different majors. He stayed an extra quarter and took a couple of other classes. We lived across the hall from each other in the fraternity house. And we lived together in an apartment along with two other friends our senior year.

We even shared a dog we named Larry. We had seen a sign advertising free puppies, and we thought we needed a watch dog for our apartment. Much to the consternation of our other roommates, we brought a brand new puppy back to the apartment. Larry was the only college educated dog I ever met. We would take turns taking Larry home on the weekends we went home. Sometimes Larry would go to Stone Mountain. And sometimes he would go to Reynolds. After we graduated, we literally flipped a coin to see who Larry would live with permanently. I won that coin toss. Larry moved to Reynolds with me after I graduated and ended up getting run over by the city garbage truck.

I don't remember exactly how it came about, but Tim and I went together one night to pick up blind dates. Not that they were really blind but we had never met either one of them. Tim introduced himself that night as Bruce. I introduced myself as Tim. And we went by those names the entire evening. I was supposed to have a date with a girl named Barbara, and Tim was supposed to have a date with the other girl (I forget her name). Tim, who called himself Bruce, ended up with Barbara. I, who called myself Tim, ended up with the other girl. A few days later Tim explained to Barbara that he really was not Bruce. It was a tough explanation to make. But it must have worked. Tim ended up marrying Barbara about 2 years later. I never saw the other girl again.

I could write a book on my time at UGA. Maybe one day I will. Tim would be in most of the pages of that book. It was a marvelous four years and a part of my life I will never forget. Not surprisingly, after spending so much time together during our college years, Tim and I didn't see each other very often after we graduated. We lived in different parts of the state and moved on with life and began raising our families. But we did stay in touch. We would talk a few times a year, and we made a point to visit whenever we could. And when we visited we could easily pick up right where we left off last time. Most of that time together was laughing about some of the crazy stuff we did, but as I look back now the visits were not nearly enough.

Several years ago I got a call that Tim had been in a freak accident and did not make it. That afternoon I suddenly found myself at their home and the next day after that I found myself serving as a pallbearer and delivering the eulogy at his funeral. Tim's death rocked my world.

But my grief could not even be compared to what Barbara, Andy, Katy, Timmy and the rest of this family were going through. Tim was very much a people person and was so full of life. One minute he was here. The next minute he was gone. And this family was forced to walk down the most difficult path this life can take.

But just as Tim would have wanted it, this family kept living their lives. I saw that last night. There are two grandchildren now, and a daughter-in-law and a son-in-law. As I visited Barbara and these now grown kids last night, I saw so much of Tim. I was reminded that Tim may be gone physically but he is very much alive in these kids. It was like I was visiting with Tim all over again. And that is exactly the way it is supposed to be. I left with a lump in my throat because of all the memories. But I also had a smile on my face because of the way they continue to live life.

Of this I am absolutely certain.

Tim would be extremely proud.

May 27, 2007

It's Up to Ariel Now

(Hayden, Ala.) So you think you've had a rough day? Or week? Or year? Hopefully it has not been as rough as it has been on the families and friends of three teenage girls who were killed in an automobile wreck near here about six months ago. And hopefully not as rough as it has been on the four teenage occupants that survived that horrific accident.

I met one of those girls tonight. A co-worker and I stopped in a barbecue restaurant off I-65 north of Birmingham to get a bite to eat. When I walked in the door of the restaurant, I noticed a large picture on the wall of a very cute girl who was obviously a former employee. There was also a plaque in her memory as well as a couple of jerseys hanging on the wall.

When we sat down at our table a waitress by the name of Ariel walked up to our table and said she would be taking care of us. Before we could say "iced tea," I asked her about the girl named Courtney Nicely I had just read about when I walked into the restaurant.

Ariel's expression changed quickly as soon as I asked the question. She began to tell us the story of seven cheerleaders from Hayden High who were returning from cheerleader competition practice last November. The girls were singing and dancing and enjoying being girls when the car suddenly went off the road, hit a tree and went down a steep bank. The three girls in the front seat lived. Three of the four girls in the back seat died.

Ariel was in the backseat.

Ariel went on to tell us that she and Courtney were best friends – joined at the hip. Ariel had back surgery as a result of that accident and although you would never know it by the way she walks and works, she told us she still experiences pain.

It is also obvious she experiences other pain that has nothing to do with her back.

But Ariel has chosen to keep moving and live her life – in spite of this heart wrenching tragedy. She plans on attending the University of Alabama in the fall. When she gets there she will find that she has a different perspective from most college freshmen. And that perspective was learned the most difficult way one can be taught.

I don't know what else Ariel will have to face in life, but I have a feeling she will be able to handle most anything thrown at her.

Ariel told me that she and Courtney did the announcements at school every morning. Courtney always signed off on the PA with these words; "Go out and have a great day!" She would pause and add these words; "Or not. It is up to you."

There is no doubt that Courtney's words are ringing in Ariel's ears these days. And she is heeding her late best friend's advice.

It's up to Ariel now. And I have a feeling that one day at a time, Ariel is choosing to have a great day.

God be with her. And God be with the parents, the families and all the friends of those who died.

Go out and have a great day or not. It is up to you.

May 28, 2008

Live Ahead of the Curve

Today, I called a friend who was just diagnosed with a brain tumor. She will have surgery to remove as much of the tumor as they can. But they know they cannot get it all. She told me the good news is that the tumor is contained in the brain, if you can call that good news. The bad news is they feel certain it will come back. But hopefully the surgery will prolong her life. Three months, six months, maybe even years. Who knows for sure?

What I do know for sure is life can throw us curves. We just never know from day to day what we will be facing next. I can tell you my friend had no idea last Thursday that she would be having brain surgery the next Thursday

A few minutes after having that grueling conversation a voice message was left on my cell phone giving me the news about another friend who had a heart attack today. She is a 45 year old fun loving gal who is about as full of life as one can get. And one who looks a picture of health. The last word I got today was, the doctors were trying to determine if they could do a stent or would have to do bypass surgery.

I can tell you when my friend was at church on Easter Sunday she did not have on her calendar to be in cardiac intensive care on Tuesday.

We just never know what we will be facing from one day to the next. One minute all can seem to be perfect. The next minute the walls can be falling down around us.

Life can definitely throw us some major curves.

Maybe it would be a good idea to stop and smell the roses while your smeller works. If you like to fish, maybe you should make time to wet a hook. Maybe you have a friend you have not visited in a long time. Maybe it would be a good thing to go for a visit or make that call. Or take a trip with your family.

At the very least maybe we should not make mountains out of molehills. Maybe we should be a little more forgiving to folks who don't do it just right. Maybe we should lighten up a little and spend more time hanging around folks who make us laugh and who love us in spite of ourselves. Maybe we should not take ourselves so seriously.

The curves will continue to come. That is for sure.

If only we could just learn to live ahead of the curve.

March 25, 2008

Some Things Are Relative

I am one of those people who strongly believe in absolute truths. I think one of the problems we have in America is many people see truth as relative. In other words, truth is true only under certain conditions. We can go down the wrong path in a hurry with such thinking.

But with that said, some truth is definitely relative. For instance at almost 6 feet 5 inches I am considered a tall guy. But when I stand next to 7 foot 2 inch former NBA star Tree Rollins as I did last night, I am not tall at all.

Being tall is relative.

During the CB radio craze of the 1970's, my handle was Big Foot – named appropriately for my number 14's. When I placed my foot next to Tree's number 18's, a more appropriate handle for me would be "Little Foot."

Shoe size is definitely relative.

Being overweight is also relative. I have noticed my pants have gotten a little tighter recently, and I don't think it is because the pants are getting smaller. Stops at places like the AQ Chicken House in Springdale, Ark. where I ate some of the best fried-chicken does not help. But the person who sat next to me (and on me) last week on a flight from Northwest Arkansas to Atlanta made me look skinny and feel skinny. Additionally, he caused me to get really spiritual, because I was thanking God when I got off that plane.

Pain is also relative.

I have a strong feeling that my wife will be experiencing a lot of that this time tomorrow night. She is scheduled for surgery tomorrow. The surgeon has already warned her that after he fixes the deviated septum in her nose she will hate his guts for several days. I think I will get the photo of Tree and me framed and place it beside her bed so she can be reminded during her recovery that her pain is relative.

Somewhere there will be someone recuperating from hemorrhoid surgery.

February 19, 2008

A Lot Can Change in a Week

We attended a baby shower from heaven tonight. And it was the kind of shower that waters your soul and "yields seed for the sower and bread for the eater."

Just a week ago Kevin and Wendy, our friends and members of our church home group, were at the end of their rope and walking through one of the most painful experiences life can throw at you.

After years of suffering through the pain of not having a baby, they had decided to go the route of adoption. They jumped through all the hoops and had done all that is necessary to be qualified to get on a list to adopt a baby. Out of the clear blue they got a call and a birth mother in another state had chosen them to be the parents of a little girl. As you could imagine Kevin and Wendy were past excited, and their family and friends were excited with them.

They had only a few days of preparation and all of a sudden they got word that the birth mother was in labor. Sparing you all the hectic details, they flew across the country at a moment's notice to be at the hospital for their baby to be born. The little girl they had prayed for came, and she was beautiful and healthy. But things started to go downhill quickly in the nursery at the hospital.

The little girl they had waited on for so long started to struggle to breathe and suddenly died. Utter joy and excitement quickly turned to utter despair and devastation.

But in spite of their pain, when they returned home Kevin and Wendy were determined that their faith would not be shaken. And their blood family and church family were also determined that they would not let them let their faith be shaken. To say that a lot of prayers were lifted to heaven for Kevin and Wendy would be a huge understatement. Heaven was bombarded on behalf of this couple.

The prayers were answered in short order. Kevin and Wendy got a call this week with the news that they have been chosen by another birth mother to adopt a little girl who will be born in less than two weeks. I'm not sure how the adoptive process works, but I am fairly certain that birth mother number 2 did not know what this couple has been through the last two weeks.

Incredibly, utter despair and devastation turned quickly back to utter joy and excitement.

I don't pretend to know the odds of this couple being chosen twice in a two week period to be adoptive parents, but I would think they would not be good. I do know people who stay on that list a long time and never get chosen to be parents.

There are definitely a lot of things I don't understand.

But what I do understand is that we attended a baby shower from heaven tonight. And I also understand that no matter how bad or dark or hopeless your situation may seem, the God who is in Heaven can turn the bad into good, the darkness into light and the hopelessness to hope.

And He can do it in an instant.

Last Sunday night, Kevin and Wendy met with their church home group in an attempt to cope with the greatest pain they had ever experienced in life. Tonight they met with that same group to celebrate the soon-to-be birth of their daughter.

My goodness a lot can change in a week.

January 27, 2008

I Beg Your Pardon

I speak about it all the time. It is not one of those things that I believe to be true.

This is one of those things that I know to be true.

In this world we will have trouble. The sun comes up – it goes down. Day and night happens every single day. Rain comes and then the sun comes out. Life is a cycle. The bottom line is that we are either about to go through trouble, in the middle of trouble or just walked out of it… and the cycle begins again.

Remember that song by the country music artist Lynn Anderson? "I beg your pardon. I never promised you a rose garden."

I think she was right.

Although we know all that to be true, we still are shocked and paralyzed when the walls start falling down around us. Or the wheels begin to come off. We are human. We hurt and ache and feel despair and feel sorry for ourselves.

And then we meet someone who has it much worse.

Christmas eve I visited with an old friend, Jerry Morrow, who was diagnosed about a year ago with Lou Gehrig Disease. His body is failing, and he knows it. But his attitude is only getting stronger. And he inspires those who are privileged to be in his presence.

During our conversation, he hands me a newspaper article about his amazing son, Duane, who had a spinal cord injury a couple of years ago that left him without use of his limbs. The front page article was about how he responded to the injury, and became a world class wheelchair athlete and continues to work, spend time with his family and live a normal life in spite of his tragedy.

Today, I talked to a friend from California who got news this weekend that her daughter had been shot and killed. She tried to explain the circumstances, but I really didn't hear her. But I did hear her very plainly when she said, "I will continue to trust God in spite of my pain."

The truth is no matter how bad we think we have it, somebody has it worse. And no matter how we handle our trouble, it is not difficult to find others who are handling their trouble much better.

Through it all, we have an opportunity to grow as human beings, and maybe we even get to find out if the faith we profess is really genuine.

December 27, 2007

He Never Lets Go

Phillip McMinn and his wife Phyllis came to Reynolds right out of seminary. The First Baptist Church of Reynolds would be his first church. I was not a member of his church, but we quickly became friends. As the local undertaker, I worked with him often. It was obvious to me having listened to many funeral sermons that Phillip had a real gift. He was very smart and had the gift of communication. He also had a heart for people, a passion for the ministry and a great sense of humor.

Most church people around Reynolds knew this gifted young preacher was on his way up. In other words, we knew a bigger church in a bigger town would grab him, and he would be on his way. Reynolds and the local Baptist church were fortunate to have him and Phyllis for six years.

As I did with most of the good preachers who left Reynolds and Taylor County for other ministries in other places, I continued to stay in touch with Phil because families would ask me to call him back to speak at funerals. I kept the addresses of several former preachers, because I knew the day would come when I would be asked to contact them. I think Phil came back more than all the others. He made that kind of impact on folks. In fact, I was told yesterday that Phil was in Reynolds just a couple of weeks ago to preach a funeral. He has been gone for over 15 years. That says something about Phil McMinn.

Since I was also in the furniture business, I sold Phillip some office furniture for his new church after he left Reynolds. A few years ago I spoke at a banquet at his church in Lawrenceville, Ga. Last year I spoke for a medical group in Greenwood, S.C. I didn't realize until I got there that Phil was the new pastor of South Main Street Baptist Church in Greenwood, and he had recommended me for that engagement. Although he was out of town the night I was there, I figured that one day I would get a call from Phil to go back to Greenwood to speak to a special event at his growing church, or at least I hoped so.

That call won't be coming.

I got a call from my brother this afternoon telling me that Phil had been killed in an automobile accident, but he knew no details. Before I could get my breath, I got an email from a friend I met in Greenwood who is a deacon at South Main Street Church.

Phil was returning alone from a Staff-Deacon retreat early Saturday afternoon. He apparently ran off the right side of the road, over compensated and lost control of his car.

And in an instant his wife of 27 years and four beautiful children had their hearts ripped out, and their lives turned upside down. And so did his 1,200 member and growing congregation at South Main Street Baptist Church.

I have been reminded again that we are not promised our next breath. Phil had been meeting with his deacons and staff planning the next steps for their church.

Today they were planning his funeral.

I don't pretend to understand the ways of God. Phil was definitely one of God's true ambassadors. He was at the peak of his life and the possibilities for him, his family and ministry were limitless. But God apparently had other plans.

In spite of our limited understanding, God is still in control.

He never lets go.

October 21, 2007

Houston's Best

(Houston, Texas) I met Jim Toney a couple of years ago. I was at our corporate office in Houston and had to get to the airport. I hurriedly got in the backseat of a car and immediately noticed something different.

For starters the driver spoke English. I thought that was a little unusual. He also was wearing a tie. I started to look around, and I noticed how clean the automobile was inside. There were current magazines on the holder on the seat in front of me. There was also a copy of that day's paper.

My curiosity was in gear by now, so I started asking him questions. It was obvious to me that Jim was not your usual cab driver.

When we got to the airport, Jim gave me his card that had his cell number and his email address. I also noticed he was carrying a Blackberry. He told me the next time I was coming to Houston to give him a call or shoot him an email, and he would pick me up.

That was a couple of years ago. He has now picked me up dozens of times as he did last night when I arrived in Houston.

For the record, Jim has two bachelor degrees from the University of Houston. He has a degree in Mathematics and a separate degree in Environmental Science. This scientist turned chauffeur worked in the oil industry for years and also was in the semiconductor industry.

I have asked him why he is doing this job since he is qualified to do much more. His answer is simple: "To keep a roof over my head and food on the table."

He works seven days a week. Like most in the service business, he has built his business by building relationships with his clients. Most of his business is repeat business like mine. People call him when they are coming to town because he offers what most other drivers don't, such as dependability, personal hygiene and the English language.

He also offers some very interesting conversation.

There is a moral to this story, and I think about it every time I get in the car with Jim Toney.

Sometimes we just have to do what we have to do.

We have two options: We can complain and fuss and wonder why. Or we can make the most of whatever situation we find ourselves and move on down the road.

Jim chose the latter.

I don't know what kind of scientist he was in his former life. But he is the best chauffeur Houston has to offer.

November 11, 2006

Other Than That, It Went Fine

Deanne Collis is like a daughter to us. I was bragging to someone today about how far she has come in life and about the fact that she was about to begin her pursuit of her Master of Science in Radiological Sciences.

She told me recently she will be pursuing her degree online but would have to go out to Wichita Falls, Texas once every six weeks or so to meet in the classroom and take exams.

She was not excited at all about flying and mentioned that Brian (her husband) would go with her the first time because she was nervous about traveling that far by herself, and she was not excited about flying on an airplane.

I reassured her that all would be fine and flying is a piece of cake.

I have a feeling she thinks I lied.

I was forwarded an email last night written by Dee about her first trip to Texas recently.

I couldn't help but laugh.

It could only happen to her.

I think you will appreciate it more if I give you an excerpt from her email. She began by talking about the fact that she did complete the first trip to Texas successfully. And I quote:

The flight out there and back was a nightmare though. The airplane left late from Atlanta, caused us to miss the connecting flight in Dallas, then they made us get and pay for a hotel. We left the next morning and then the airlines lost our luggage! I had to go to the first day of grad school in the same clothes I had worn and slept in for 2 days! You know me, I was trying to salvage what make-up and mascara I had on my face but it was pretty hard through all the tears and crying! I HATE FLYING! I did buy a little make-up to do some "touch up" but it didn't help much. I couldn't wash my hair because I didn't have my straight iron and if I had washed it I would have looked like I stuck my hand in a light socket. So I tried to sleep without moving my head. It was awful!! Brian was over in his bed, at the hotel, doing the same thing! And he didn't have anywhere to go or be! Then of course, they wanted to take pictures to make student ID's on that very day. Lord, my picture looks like crap and will be a constant reminder for the next 2 years of the day from "you know where!" Other than that it went fine.

I guess I should give her a call and tell her she has experienced most everything that can go wrong on a trip, so it should be downhill for her from here.

But I probably shouldn't tell her that the airlines lost my luggage on three consecutive trips a year or two ago. And I can't tell her the number of times they have lost my shaving kit that was in my suitcase. Nor will I tell her about the time I sat next to the huge man that had obviously eaten too many beans the night before. Nor will I tell her about the rainy night when the plane I was riding in got within feet of landing and took back off again. I surely will not mention how many hours I've sat in airports waiting on delayed planes. And I can't tell her about the time I checked in a hotel, unlocked the room door with my key and noticed a pair of ladies undergarments on the floor and an un-made bed.

But I will have to admit that through all my traveling I don't think I have ever tried to sleep without moving my head.

September 26, 2006

Miracle Could Be Waiting

The Crawley's lived in a big two story house right across the street from the Methodist Church. Mr. Crawley was a local attorney and Mrs. Crawley was a schoolteacher. They raised four children, including twins. Mrs. Crawley started a kindergarten somewhere around 1959, and I was fortunate enough to attend that school for a year.

The group that attended that kindergarten has continued to be friends throughout the years. We don't see each other often but when we do we pick right up where we left off last. We have common roots.

Will and Mike Crawley were part of that group and have always been very close friends of mine. They are identical twins and were born a couple of weeks after me. I went through 12 years of school with them, and we have stayed in touch through the years.

The Crawley twins grew to be big strong, burly guys. Somebody nicknamed them Big Hippo and Little Hippo. Everybody knows the Hippo brothers. They definitely made their mark on central Georgia as they were reaching for adulthood.

Mike has worked at the Medical Center in Macon for years. He started as a Paramedic with the ambulance service there and ended up becoming a Registered Nurse. Everybody at the Medical Center knows Mike Crawley.

A number of years ago Mike had back surgery. Mike came to Reynolds to recuperate, and there was a period of time that Mike could not get out of bed on his own. I went by the house at least twice a day to help get him up so he could walk as was required for his recovery.

Several years later I got a call from Will that Mike was about to have heart bypass surgery. I left immediately for the hospital and waited in the waiting room with their family until we heard from the doctors and knew he was okay.

Just making the point about our lifelong friendship.

And why the rest of this story is important to me.

Will left college to start a landscaping business. He successfully ran that business for many years. A few years ago, Will began to have some physical problems. Because of some strange hereditary reason, his liver went bad.

I made it my business to stay in touch with him and made trips to Reynolds as often as possible to visit with him and check on him. There were many people in Reynolds who rallied around him during this time.

His twin brother Mike was amazing during that illness. He looked after his brother. And he used every resource available to him to do everything he could to make sure his brother had a chance to get better.

It did not look good. Every visit to Reynolds I could tell Will was getting worse. I knew unless a miracle happened he would not be with us long.

During his illness Will became an inspiration to many. He never gave up and always kept an upbeat attitude. He also developed a strong faith and his faith made everybody around him stronger.

But I knew in my heart unless a miracle happened he would not be with us much longer.

The miracle happened.

Through the grace of God and a persistent brother in the medical field, Will received a liver transplant. I visited him at Emory University Hospital a couple of days after that transplant. I found out during that visit that Will had gotten back on his feet as quickly as anyone who had that surgery at Emory Hospital.

He was a new person. And just as his health declined so quickly for months on end, now his health was improving just that quickly.

I saw him at a wedding a few weeks ago, and he asked me to feel the muscle in his arm. It was as hard as a rock. I couldn't help remember that just a few short months ago he was as weak as one could be.

Will also decided to go back to school and finish his college education and get his degree. And he is pursuing that now just as hard as he pursued getting well when nobody gave him much of a chance.

Will is a walking miracle. And he is very grateful for another shot at life.

There is a lesson here for all of us.

No matter how hopeless our situation and helpless we feel about it, we never should lose hope.

And we should never give up.

You never know.

When we least expect it a miracle could be waiting right around the corner.

September 3, 2006

Note: On February 1, 2007, Will's twin brother, Mike, died after a courageous fight with liver cancer. The irony is that Will, who we thought would not make it, is doing fine. And Mike, who was doing fine, passed away. Will Crawley not only completed his college degree but he has now completed his Masters in Public Health. Mike was inspired as he watched his brother receive a miracle and was a new man with a new found faith when he died. Mike saved Will's life with his determination to make sure he got a liver.... and in the end Will might have saved his brother's life as well.

Basket Two

Squeezing Life

"Eulan Brown chose to live one day at a time. He lived in the moment. He did not spend his energy worrying about what happened yesterday or what caused his plight in life. And he surely didn't concern himself with what would or could happen tomorrow. He just squeezed all he could out of each day."

True in Golf - True in Life

I wonder how many people ever saw a rabbit running loose on a golf course? Wade Lane saw many of them and at the end of the day he usually had a few in his pocket.

For you folks not in the know, a "rabbit" is a way keeping score. It was worth a one dollar bill at the Reynolds Golf Course. You let the imaginary rabbit go on the first tee. You caught him when you won a hole outright. That means you had to beat everybody else in your foursome on that hole. If someone else won the next hole the rabbit would be loose again. If you won two holes in a row you would have a rabbit and a leg. Now it became a little more difficult for your opponents to set him loose again.

Every now and then an opponent would set another rabbit loose… and maybe even another. There would be rabbits running all over the place.

And you needed an accountant to keep up with all the rabbits and legs and dollar bills.

But Wade was hard to beat. And most of the time he beat you with his putter. Nobody putted like Wade Lane.

His usual comment: "It's not how you drive, but how you arrive."

I had some amusing moments on several occasions on the last tee when my dad and Wade would be arguing over who had which rabbits. At that point in their life, neither of them could hear very well. So in other words, daddy might have let another rabbit loose, and Wade didn't exactly hear him when he let him loose… or vice versa.

A stranger could have heard those two and thought they were enemies. The truth is they would leave the golf course, go pick up their wives and all go to dinner together.

I remember one afternoon there were at least five of us playing together. We were about to play our third round, and everybody hit the ball off the first tee. Everybody went to their ball to get ready for their second shot, but Wade could not find his ball. He always hit the ball straight down the middle so everybody was puzzled that his ball could not be found. After a five minute group effort to find Wade's ball, he came up with a rather interesting comment.

"You know what? I don't believe I ever teed off!"

And he hadn't. He went back to the tee to hit his ball.

You can surmise that there was more conversation going on than golfing.

Wade and I were partners more than a few times in local golf tournaments. He was the best partner you could have in a scramble format golf tournament because of his putting. If the ball was anywhere close to the hole, he would drain it.

Wade was also the king of Irritable Bowel Syndrome. You can take that from someone who knows more than a little about that subject. He always carried a roll of toilet paper in his golf bag. We were playing together in a tournament one weekend, and were about to hit our approach shot on the first hole. The other pair in our foursome was from out of town and complete strangers to us. We met them on the first tee.

All of a sudden Wade jumped out of the golf cart and dug in his golf bag for his Charmin and headed for the woods. The startled strangers asked me if he was okay. We watched Wade hurriedly walking in the woods. He walked so far in the woods following a path that he unknowingly came back around in our sight. He backed up and his fanny was in full view of all three of us. After he finished, he walked back through the woods and out the same path he entered.

He had no idea the show he put on for the three of us waiting in the golf carts in the fairway.

I told him what had happened on the next hole. He got a good laugh out of it. Then he lined up a 20 foot putt and nailed it.

I vividly remember the day Wade died in 1992. I went over to the Lane house in the hearse. Daddy was at the house when I got there. As I was rolling the stretcher out of the house I happened to look up at my dad. There was a huge tear rolling down his cheek.

I was reminded that day that all the hours they spent together on the golf course had nothing to do with rabbits and rabbit legs and dollar bills.

But it was about fun and fellowship and friendship.

By the way, at his family's request, I appropriately placed Wade's putter in the casket with him before he was laid to rest at Hillcrest Cemetery in Reynolds.

I can tell you that putter was not placed there as a symbol of how well he finished a hole on a golf course.

But it was placed there as a symbol of how well he finished his life.

It's not how you drive – but it's how you arrive.

True in golf and true in life.

August 28, 2006

The Pursuit of Happyness

We hold these truths to be self-evident, that all men are created equal, that they are endowed, by their Creator with certain unalienable rights, that among these are life, liberty, and the pursuit of happiness.

As you know, these words are out of the Declaration of Independence. They are also right out of a movie we went to see tonight. "The Pursuit of Happyness," starring Will Smith, is a movie worth going to see.

The movie is based on the true story of the life of Chris Gardner who literally lived on the streets of San Francisco with his toddler son while pursuing a job as a stockbroker with Dean Witter. Somehow he made it.

In fact, he made it big time.

This is one of those movies that causes one to think. That has to be a good thing.

It is interesting to me that the Declaration of Independence does not promise us the right to be happy. But it does say we all have the right to pursue happiness.

There is a difference.

In my opinion most people are not pursuing happiness. In fact, I think the majority of people are not in pursuit of anything. Most people are living their lives just to get by and have pretty much thrown the towel in on their unalienable right to pursue happiness.

They go to work, come home in the afternoon and sit in their chair and watch television. They get up the next morning and go to work doing the same thing and come home in the afternoon and do the same thing.

They live with people they don't even like and pretty much make everybody around them miserable. Maybe they have been knocked down so many times that they finally have given up.

As a lifelong undertaker, I am keenly aware that we have only one shot at this thing we call life, and we are absolutely nuts if we are not pursuing happiness with everything that is in us.

Pursuing happiness means actively building relationships with other people. Pursuing happiness means doing things that will make others around us happy. Pursuing happiness means spending quality time with our children and our families. Pursuing happiness means trying to be the best we can be at whatever it is we have been asked to do. Pursuing happiness means having a sense of humor so that others enjoy being around us. Pursuing happiness means giving to those who are less fortunate. Pursuing happiness means working harder than everyone else. Pursuing happiness means making sure we have balance in our life. Pursuing happiness means having priorities in life. Pursuing happiness means we are relentless in our attempt to understand the true meaning of life.

In my opinion, pursuing happiness is finding out what God put us on earth to do and going after it with every fiber of our being.

The message of the movie we saw tonight was that the pursuit of happiness comes with blood, sweat and tears. It is not a defensive lifestyle as most people lead, but a lifestyle of being on a mission.

None of us have an unalienable right to be happy. The truth is there will be many times when we are not.

But we do have the right to pursue it.

I think this time of the year is the perfect time to step up the pursuit.

December 18, 2006

Abby the Golf Dog

We moved out to the Reynolds Golf Course in October of 1987. A little over a year after that we brought a little Yellow Lab puppy home for our kids that would become not only a wonderful family pet but would also become somewhat of a legend at the golf course. We lived next to Number 9 fairway for 16 years. Abby was there for 15 of those years.

No doubt Abby would have made a great retriever on a dove field. But instead she became a golf ball retriever and everybody that played golf in Reynolds knew her well.

Her days were spent on the golf course, and she was trained by all the golfers.

You could hit balls as long as you wanted, and she would bring the ball back and drop it down for you to hit again.

She knew the golf course as well as anyone playing. And she also had golf etiquette. She would quit panting when you were addressing the ball and when you finished putting she would walk to the next tee to wait on you.

She also would dive for a ball in any of the ponds to retrieve your ball. She would literally disappear under water… sometimes she would come up with a mouth full of balls.

I saw many a golfer arguing on the first hole when a golfer would be convinced his opponent hit the ball in the water but when they got there the ball would be sitting in the middle of the fairway.

Abby would watch the golfers tee-off, and she played favorites. She always looked after her owner. If I was playing with three other folks and two of us hit the ball in the water, she would always retrieve my ball to give me the advantage. My opponent's ball would still be in the water.

If a golfer was not nice to her, she would take his ball out of the fairway and drop it in the water.

Many times if I was riding in a cart she would pick up golf balls that may have been in the middle of the fairway and bring them to me and drop them in my cart. I tried to break her from that . . . But I didn't try too hard. I always had plenty of golf balls. There is no telling how many golf balls were under our carport.

She usually slept with at least two golf balls in her mouth. I'm serious. I think she had a thing for golf balls.

Ed Cooper, who ran the golf course during those years, used her to retrieve balls from the ponds, and he would re-sell the balls in the pro shop. At least once a week, he took her out to dive for balls in the ponds.

He had fifty cent balls and dollar balls in two jars. And 90 percent of them were retrieved by Abby.

We moved to Warner Robins when Abby was too old to enjoy golf anymore. She lived out her last days in a strange land. Kathy called me the morning Abby died and she was so upset I thought something had happened to one of the kids.

The *Taylor County News* ran her obituary the day after her death. In lieu of flowers, the family suggested fried chicken to be sent to the house.

Abby was cremated and her ashes are in an urn on our bookcase in our den. There is a likeness of her in statue form attached to the top of the urn. Her little memorial not only gives me many opportunities to tell others about our amazing Abby, but more importantly it gives me opportunity to recall and share some wonderful memories I shared with my dad, my boys, my brothers, my friends and my dad's friends at the Reynolds Golf Course.

It doesn't take long to lose the smell of a new car, and we eventually trade it in for another. We get too fat for our favorite pants and have to buy new ones. Our furniture wears out and carpet has to be replaced. The value goes down in those things over time.

But great memories increase in value as we get older.

Abby's urn and statue always reminds me of that.

But you know what?

We never did get the first piece of fried chicken.

August 31, 2006

Lessons I Never Forgot

Hanson Law was born in 1900. I know that because he told me countless number of times. If he was still living he would now be almost 107 years old. He was employed at G.H. Goddard & Son for over 60 years.

I don't think Hanson missed many days work in those 60 something years, and he was never late for work.

A lot of us could learn a lot from a man with that kind of work ethic.

Hanson worked for my great-grandfather, my grandfather and my father. He even worked for me for a few years. He worked in the grocery store and the meat market. When daddy was in the well digging business, Hanson helped him dig wells.

He also dug more than a few graves.

When my dad's brother became ill, Hanson looked after him. He did that until the day my uncle died. Hanson did whatever needed doing at G.H.Goddard & Son store.

Everybody in Reynolds knew Hanson and everybody loved him.

Especially my dad.

There was an incident that happened at our store one Saturday night in the early sixties. To be honest, I don't know if I was there or not. I heard the story so many times it sure seems like I was there.

A local man who was obviously intoxicated came in the store that night at about closing. Hanson was waiting on him at the meat counter. The man was cussing and being loud and obnoxious as some drunks do. Daddy was watching him and watching the whole situation and could tell that Hanson was getting upset at the way the man was acting and treating him.

Remember these were the days when public restrooms had a particular sign on them that limited who could enter them based on race.

These were also the days that when we went to the movie theater in Fort Valley, the whites would sit on the main floor and the blacks would sit in the balcony.

Some of you remember well what I am talking about.

Anyway, the intoxicated redneck got louder and louder and cursed Hanson. And he used the "N" word in addressing him.

Daddy, who was much of a man in those days, walked over and grabbed the drunk by the collar and dragged him to the front of the store and literally threw him out the door onto the sidewalk with these parting words, "Don't ever step your foot in this store again."

The man took Daddy at his word and never shopped in our store again. In fact, his entire family never shopped there again and that family never used our funeral home again. Generations later that family still did not do business with our family.

I learned two lessons from that story that I have carried with me all my life:

The first is living by principles is more important than making money. Some business in not worth having.

The second lesson is we have a duty to do whatever is in our power to protect the oppressed.

I never forgot that story. For the record, I don't ever remember Daddy telling me about that night. But Hanson told me the story over and over again.

Obviously he never forgot it either.

January 7, 2007

Cannot Be Contained in a Box

The children of Irene Underwood and the late Ralph Underwood converged on Reynolds this weekend to close another chapter in their book of life. And since I married into this family over 31 years ago, their chapter is also my chapter.

As usually happens when children clean out a house that holds a lifetime of family memorabilia, things are found that are long forgotten and others that bring back tons of memories. There are some laughs and a lot of nostalgic moments. And there are a few tears. And maybe even more than a few tears when the loaded truck pulls out of the driveway for the last time.

This afternoon, when all was done, the children visited their mother who was completely oblivious to the fact that her home will be sold in a few days. I suppose sometimes the effects of Alzheimer's can be a good thing.

I have been reminded again that life on this earth is a journey, and it is a fast one at that. The physical stuff that's left behind that really matters when the destination is reached can be packed up in a few boxes and divided up between those who are left behind in a matter of a couple of days.

What cannot be contained in a box are the memories of a great life afforded to children who are left behind. In this case, four children who suddenly lost a wonderful dad when they were kids. And in this case a mom, widowed and beautiful at age 43, who chose never to get married again in order to devote her life to her children. And as a result, in this case, four children whose memories make them among the richest of any family I know.

If you are in your home reading this, look around at your furniture. Look at the pictures on the wall and china in your cabinets. There is a really good possibility that one day those you leave behind will be forced to go through all of it, throw away what they don't want and divide up whatever they decide to keep. And then there is a real possibility that a family you don't even know will move in and another story will begin.

I'm telling you it's a journey.

The only thing that matters at the end of the day are the memories you are creating wherever you are.

And thank God they don't have to be divided up, and they cannot be contained in a box.

December 28, 2008

All in a Name

It is dawning on me that you have the opportunity to read more than you ever probably wished about Reynolds and the fascinating people who made up that town during my growing up years. As I have said so many times before, I wouldn't take a million dollars for growing up in Reynolds.

I was wondering what it would be like if I could have taken each of you around town to meet some of my friends a few years ago.

I would certainly like to take you down to **Jessie Mae Koochie** King's house and introduce you to her son, **Billy Boo**. And I would love to take you by the hospital and let you meet **Bay** Humphries. I would certainly want you to meet my gorgeous sister **Kikky** and would take you across the street to **Hoot** Russell's house so you could meet his son **Brer**. I would not want you to confuse **Brer** Russell with **Bur** Montfort who lived down the street. I would also walk next door so you could meet our neighbor **Higgie** James, and hopefully we could at least talk to her brother **Booty** Weaver who had moved away. We would definitely walk across the street so you could meet the Whatley's and their youngest daughter **Tuggie**. I couldn't introduce you to **Coot** Payne because he died before I was born but you would love **Sink** Marshall who always had a practical joke to pull on someone. Maybe we could even find **Ducker** Whatley, and catch him before he moved away. If not, I'm sure we could find **Duck** Powell hanging around the police station. I would love to take you out Highway 128, so you could meet **Mud Duck** Hartley. Maybe we could even find his cousin **Beanie** while we were in the neighborhood.

If Little League Baseball was in season, I would introduce you to two of the best infielders Reynolds had to offer, **Cobby** Patterson and **Runt** Lowe. We would try to get **Dink** Hooten to drive us out to Beechwood, so you could meet **Pig** Payne. And we could circle back through Potterville, so you could meet **Fuzzy** Childree and stop by the Edmonson's to see if **Yak Yak** Youngblood happened to be visiting his in-laws.

I could take you around town and by the clothing store so you could meet **Cat** Brady. **Kitty** Beeland may be in the store shopping when we stop by. I would hope you would get to see **Son Buddy** Mathis around town. If you seemed to be having a sad day, I would take you by the bank and introduce you to **Happy** Smith.

I would love to take you the home of Lt. Governor Byrd so you could meet his son **Woochie.** And I would take you to Whatley's pond so you could meet Harold Helm's wife, **Wootie.** Actually before we drove to the pond, we would drop by **Doodum** Goodwin's house so you could buy some worms. After thinking about it, while we were at the Byrd's house, it would be nice if they could help us call Sen. Talmadge's office in Washington so we could speak to **Tac** Brunson, who was also from Reynolds. We would have to go out by the golf course so you could meet **Snookie** Harrell and drive by Hobbsville so you could meet **Snook** Hobbs. And we certainly couldn't leave Reynolds unless you met the Crawley twins, who were known as **Big Hippo** and **Little Hippo**.

On the way out of town we would have to stop by Sydney Bryan's farm and meet **Peter Rat, Thirteen, Jaypan, Big Head, Yoke, Cheese** and **Bennie Bird.**

As we headed back home you would probably ask me how the people of Reynolds got such names. I'm sure I could have explained it somehow.

I don't think I would have ever had the nerve tell you that everybody called me **Lucy.**

July 16, 2006

A Hug is Worth a Thousand Words

I first met Ed Grisamore about 10 years ago as I was getting in my car after I had spoken at a civic club in Macon. I had actually already met him in print because I was already reading his column in the *Macon Telegraph* on a regular basis. He told me he would like to come to Reynolds and interview me for a column.

I was flattered but kind of nervous at the same time. Not nervous because he wanted to do an interview but I was nervous because I didn't know the slant he would put on my humorous slant of the funeral business. The last thing I wanted was for someone to take my humor the wrong way, and I knew that could happen if I was not in control of what would be written.

He came over and we sat on the front porch of the funeral home in Reynolds. He asked me questions, and I answered them. And I probably answered some questions he didn't ask. We realized we had a lot in common and really hit it off.

A special friendship had begun.

The article came out in the next day or two and his slant was perfect. Because of his article, the demand for my speaking services increased at an almost alarming rate. No doubt about it, Ed Grisamore put me on the map with that article.

I was always completely fascinated by Ed's writing ability. He paints an amazing picture with words and his columns are always positive and motivating and heart-warming. He has brightened the day for many folks in Middle Georgia for many years.

I am one of them.

He encouraged me over and over to put my own stories in writing and actually wrote the foreword to my first book.

Ed and I have continued our friendship since the first time we met. We make it a point to meet for lunch every now and then to catch up and enjoy each other's company.

If you read Ed's columns or have read his books, you know about the close relationship he had with his dad. I met Ed's dad and mom at the book signing when Ed's first book was released. I feel like I knew Ed's dad well because I have read the words Ed has written about him. I have also heard Ed speak so affectionately of him many times.

Ed's dad, Jennings M. Grisamore, MD, died a few weeks ago. His memorial service was held today. I was there.

I had several impressions as I sat in the congregation. My first impression was that Ed Grisamore's dad was an amazing human being. Secondly, as I listened to what this man accomplished in life, I realized that Ed has been very humble in talking about his dad. And my third impression was that this man produced an exceptional family.

As I sat and listened, I had to fight back tears. I fought tears because I was getting a glimpse of the impact one man can have on people in his care. I fought tears because the service brought back memories of my own dad who impacted me so greatly. I fought back tears because I never want to lose sight of the important things in life. You can't attend a service like that without doing some inner soul searching.

After the service, I worked my way through the crowd of people at the reception and found Ed. There was really nothing to say. I hugged him; he hugged me back; and we shed tears.

I left that reception with another impression.

A hug is worth a thousand words.

A real friend is worth more.

November 26, 2006

"Your People Shall Be My People"

I got a call from my youngest son about midnight this past Tuesday. He was calling to tell me that Jessie Mae King was in the hospital and was very sick. She has been part of our family since about 12 years before I was born. When I got married and started having children she came out of retirement and helped raise my boys. And my boys consider her another Grandma. She turned 100 a couple of months ago, so when she gets admitted to the hospital it gets our attention.

I visited her yesterday in the hospital. I walked into the room, and I was surprised that she called my name. Her mental clarity is not what it used to be. She calls me Brucie. She was brought by ambulance to the hospital this week because they could not wake her up. I'm not sure of the extent of her other problems, but they did discover she has congestive heart failure. But not surprisingly, she has come back strong. Hopefully, she will be dismissed from the hospital today.

Jessie has three living children. She lives with her son Billy and his wife Jeanette in Reynolds. Billy has been ill for several years, and Jeanette not only helps look after her husband but she also looks after her mother-in-law. Today when I walked into the hospital room Jeannette was wearing gloves and had just finished changing Jessie's diaper. Jeanette has gone home only one time in the past five days. She has spent every single night in a chair by her mother-in-law's side. She waits on her hand and foot. And she was waiting on her hand and foot before she was admitted to the hospital.

I was reminded today of the biblical account of Ruth and Naomi. Naomi refused to leave her mother-in-law's side. Although most people could not understand Naomi's faithfulness to Ruth, God blessed her faithfulness in a remarkable way.

And I have a feeling God will bless this daughter-in-law's faithfulness in an exceptional way.

Maybe it's because I saw the relationship my own wife had with my mother. Or maybe it's because of the incredible daughters-in-law God has given me. But I have a special place in my heart for daughters-in-law.

Maybe that's why God gave me three sons.

May 06, 2007

Pedestrian Safety

It was spring quarter of 1976. I was really tired of school and almost done but there were a few more hours I had to get under my belt to graduate. I had a couple of courses to take and I had the privilege to choose an elective for the other.

A couple of buddies and I found just the course. It was called "Traffic Safety." This was before the Jan Kemp affair at the UGA (she exposed special academic favors for football players) and therefore during the days when they passed Georgia Bulldog athletes whether they could read or write or not.

And they had classes designed just for them.

When we discovered that the three of us would be the only students in the class that were not on the football team we knew we were in the right class.

I remember the first test we took. Questions like…if you are driving down the road and you have a flat tire you should. 1) Slam on brakes 2) Honk the horn profusely or 3) pull slowly off the road. All three of us aced that first test and we knew we had it made.

After the first test the teacher assigned a partner for each student. Each pair had to choose a topic and teach the class for the assigned 50 minutes during the quarter.

Since we were the only students in the class that were not football players he let the three of us be partners. We didn't spend a lot of time choosing our topic.

Pedestrian Safety.

We were assigned a date to teach the class for 50 minutes and had to write a paper on that topic.

There was a caveat. He expected all students to actually attend the class and we even had to sign in for each class. And there would be a final test over all the material covered by the student teachers for that class.

In other words we had to listen to the football players give lectures every day about traffic safety.

We tried attending and taking notes but it was the most boring thing we had ever sat through in our entire college experience. Since it was spring quarter and such beautiful weather, we took turns signing in for each other. In other words, we would pull up in front of the Education building and one of us would go in (wearing golf cleats) and sign the three names on the sheet and then all three of us would take off for the golf course.

We figured the final test couldn't be that hard.

On one of those beautiful Friday afternoons, my friend Tim went in to sign our names on the attendance roll as Bennett and I sat in the car.

In just a few minutes, he came running out with a funny look on his face and explained to us that they had changed the schedule and we were expected to teach that day.

Like right now. We knew the teaching assignment was weighted very heavy for our grade for the quarter. And we certainly wanted to graduate.

The three of us calmly walked into the classroom totally unprepared to teach for 50 minutes on Pedestrian Safety. None of us had done one bit of research or for that matter had even thought about the subject.

We walked in and the first thing that struck me was that all the students were in their places in their desk ready to take notes on that day's lecture.

What happened that day still causes me to laugh.

Out loud.

There is something funny about standing in front of a room full of Division I college athletes to teach a subject that we knew absolutely nothing about. And it's more than funny to realize that they are about to take notes on your lecture.

For some reason I went first.

There was a lot of stuff written on the board so I took my time erasing it. I was erasing and thinking about what in the heck I was going to talk about.

The professor finally told me I had the chalkboard erased very well and to go ahead with my lecture.

As I turned to face the audience I noticed my friend Tim. He was frantically looking through a pile of magazines he picked up when he walked in the door. I suppose he was looking for an article about pedestrians. Then I looked over at my other friend. Bennett was just as relaxed as one could be. His arms were folded looking like he was looking forward to what I had to say.

The sight of the two of them made me smile. I could only imagine what was going on in their heads.

I begin to speak right off the top of my head: "There are three basic types of pedestrians."

I was watching with amazement as the football players/students wrote down what I said. I decided to help them and wrote the same on the blackboard.

"First you've got your old people." I talked a minute or so about old people who can't hear or see and how they may walk in front of you as you are driving down the road.

"Secondly, you've got your young people." Everybody wrote that down as well so I helped them again and wrote that on the board and talked about young people who may chase a ball and run in front of a car.

I couldn't help but notice Bennett still relaxed, arms folded, seemingly totally enjoying my ridiculous presentation. I was trying not to laugh thinking about what he was going to talk about when I was finished. Tim was continuing to frantically look through those magazines.

"Thirdly," I said, "You've got your drunks." I made a few comments about drunks not knowing what they are doing and how they could stagger out in front of a car.

I finished and sat down at my desk. I had spoken for 4 minutes. We still had 46 minutes to go. And now I was about to have a stroke to keep from laughing. Especially when Bennett told me how much he enjoyed my lecture.

But so far we were still in the game or should I say the class.

Tim came up next and instead of standing to address the class, he sat at the teacher's desk at the front of the room.

He proceeded to read an article he had found. I have no idea what the article was about but I never heard the word pedestrian.

By this time I could hardly control myself in my attempt to keep from laughing.

Tim's reading lasted about three minutes. Bennett was still relaxed in his chair seemingly enjoying taking it all in.

When Tim returned to his seat, Bennett calmly stood up and walked to the front of the board. He took his time to erase what I had written on the board. He had 43 minutes of time to take up. The teacher finally told him (as he told me) that the board was erased enough and to please continue with the lecture.

Bennett finally wrote the word "Pedestrian" on the board. He misspelled it.

He wasn't even close.

I was about to lose it by now. And so was Tim.

I had my head in my arms on my desk. I couldn't look up.

Bennett then began to attempt to break the misspelled word "Pedestrian" down in syllables. PID/ES/TR/AN. The football players had now put their pens down and were wondering what was going on.

All of a sudden Bennett turned around and faced the class. He held both hands out from his sides and very calmly with much thought asked, "What can you say about Pedestrian Safety that hasn't already been said?"

I fell out of the desk. Literally. Never laughed so much in my life. I was howling and the honest truth is I am laughing as I type this. Tim was doing the same.

We had a friend who knew of our predicament and was standing in the hall watching the whole thing. I looked at her and she was bent over laughing.

By then everybody was laughing.

The teacher called the class off and sent everybody out but he asked us to stay around. Somehow, someway, we were able to talk him into letting us write the paper that weekend and present it to the class on Monday.

The three of us made a C in Traffic Safety. I can promise you everybody else in that class made an A.

Tim, Bennett and I are probably the only people in the history of UGA that made a C in Traffic Safety.

I'm sure the UGA powers-to-be took that class off the curriculum pretty quickly after Jan Kemp brought such classes to light.

But I still laugh every time I think of it.

October 17, 2006

A Tip Top Day

When the Atlanta Braves won the World Series in 1995, my good friend Ed Grisamore wrote an amazing column for the *Macon Telegraph*. That column showed up in newspapers all around the country. The article began something like this: It's hard to type with tears in your eyes.

I can relate to that statement tonight.

My middle son and his wonderful wife gave us a wonderful gift today. My wife and I officially became grandparents at 1:57 p.m.. And we will never be the same again.

Taylor Reese Goddard is more beautiful than we could ever even imagine. She has her mom's nose and her dad's mouth.

And she already has this Papa's heart.

Taylor weighed in at 7 lbs, 8 oz. Her mom and dad, although a little nervous as events began to unfold, both came through like troopers.

Two scenes are forever seared in my memory.

The first scene took place after Taylor had arrived at the nursery. We were looking through the glass as the nurse was checking her temperature, changing diapers etc. John was in the nursery standing beside the nurse staring at his little girl.

Tears were literally dripping from his eyes.

And his tears caused tears to drip from my eyes. To think that this little guy who just yesterday was playing in mud puddles and playing T-ball is now a dad almost took my breath away.

It was like the torch was passed. And I am absolutely certain that John is ready to take that torch. My son with the big heart will make an absolutely matchless dad.

The second scene took place later in the hospital room right before we left the hospital. Little Taylor was lying on her back on her little blanket on Tami's bed. Tami was staring at her little girl with her face in her hands.

Tears were literally dripping from her eyes.

Her tears caused tears to drip from my eyes. Although I understand the hormonal things that happen in a woman's body after a baby is born, there was something else happening at that moment.

The bonding of a mother and a child is the most powerful bond on earth. And it was like I was watching it take place.

We have received God's greatest blessing today. And from the bottom of our hearts we are thankful to God for the great thing He has done. He has lavished his grace on us. We didn't earn it. We didn't deserve it. But He did it anyway.

Taylor has received an unmatched blessing today. She didn't choose her wonderful parents. She had absolutely nothing to do with it. God did it. And He has lavished His grace on her.

I got an email today from my old boss and friend who now lives in Denver Colorado. He was congratulating Kathy and me for becoming grandparents. As Bob usually does, he ended his email with these words, "It's a Tip Top Day."

It really is a Tip Top Day.

Man oh man, it's a Tip Top Day.

January 24, 2007

Note: On Halloween night in 2009, our second grandchild was born in Atlanta. Anna Kathryn is the most beautiful Halloween pumpkin I've ever seen. She was born to our oldest son and his wife. David and Holly desperately wanted a child and had struggled to get pregnant. God's perfect timing was October 31, 2009. Halloween will never be the same again and neither will David and Holly. And neither will this Papa. God's grace was lavished again.

You Can Take Coach Richt's Lesson to the Bank

Mark Richt made a monumental comment in his post game interview after the Georgia – Auburn game on Saturday. *"Half the battle is energy and half the battle is execution."*

I can tell you that comment is true in football and is also true in life.

For those of you who are not SEC football fans, Coach Richt has stuck his neck out a couple of times this year in the name of energy. The first was at the Florida game when he ordered his team before the game to celebrate in the end zone after the first Georgia score. Although Florida Coach Urban Meyer was infuriated at the unusual sight, the energy created for the team, and their fans gave the Bulldogs the edge. Final score: Georgia 42 Florida 30.

Early in the week, Richt and his seniors, still trying to get the edge in a huge game, called for a "Black Out" in the game against Auburn. They asked all fans to show up at Sanford Stadium clad in black. The fans listened and turned what is normally the Red Sea into the Black Sea. It was a sight to behold.

What the fans did not know was that Richt had ordered black jersey's back in the summer for this particular game. There was speculation from the Bulldog nation that the team would be wearing black. Some were against it because the black jerseys would break the "between the hedges" tradition of red jerseys for the home team. Those fans were relieved when the team came out their pregame warm-ups wearing red. Wondering if they would change to black in the dressing room after the warm-ups, those fans were even more relieved when the captains came out to the 50 yard line for the traditional coin toss clad in red.

Then the place exploded. The Georgia team ran on the field wearing black jerseys and off came the captains' red jerseys to reveal black jersey's under them. Even Coach Richt had changed to what he called the "Johnny Cash" look. And according to some folks I talked to who were there, it may have been the most electric atmosphere ever in Sanford Stadium. There have been more than a few electric moments over the years at Sanford Stadium.

It is very true that Georgia did not win the game because of the color of their jerseys. But it was at least half the reason they won it.

I have learned in the real world there are many talented people who never have learned to win. They have the smarts and the "know how" to be the absolute best at whatever they do. But they don't have the energy or "fire in the belly" to take them to the next level.

One thing is for certain. The most talented don't always win. Talent and execution are only half the battle. The other half is energy.

And whether you are a Georgia Bulldog fan or not, you can take Coach Richt's lesson to the bank.

November 11, 2007

Always On My Mind

Dear Daddy,

Since I don't believe regular mail will make it to your mailbox these days, I will post this letter here hoping that there is a Wi-Fi wireless access somewhere in heaven where you can get online. I figure this is my best shot.

Although, I have read that one day in heaven is like a thousand years here, I am quite positive you will not take the time to do the math to figure how long ago in earth years it has been since you were promoted to your new address. Just for the record, in our timekeeping system here, it has been exactly 14 years ago today. If I am doing my math correctly, that would be about 20 minutes to you. If I live another 30 years, it would be about another 43 minutes in heaven time when we meet again.

That happens to be very encouraging to me because the things I struggle with here for a month are in reality about 7 seconds from your perspective. That means the things I struggle with for a day are like a quarter of a second from the heavenly perspective.

So I guess you are telling me I should learn to relax down here, right? I'm quite sure, with what you know now; you would tell me there is no reason for us to even sweat the big stuff, much less the small stuff.

In spite of all that Biblical and mathematical truth, I am still stuck here on the slow time. A day here is still 24 hours, and a year is 365 days. Although you haven't even had time to get your breath yet there, a lot has transpired for us here since your 20 minutes in heaven.

You had two new great grandbabies born this year (earth time). I think that makes seven for you now. If you are reading this, I'm sure you have read about little Taylor Reese. But please tell Mama (she got there about 15 seconds before you in case you haven't found her yet) that Lucy and Eric had a little girl about 3 seconds ago (your time).

You both will be very proud to know that they named her Naia after your wife and daughter and the special lady who happens to be my Mama. I am positive she will be thrilled to know that.

The odds are I will see you in about 45 minutes, but it could be quicker than that. It would suit me just fine if it is at least an hour. I would then be the ripe old age of 94.

From your perspective it certainly won't be long. Just go watch a re-run of the "Carol Burnett Show," and I'll be there.

In the meantime, please know that you were on my mind all day today. In fact you are always on my mind.

I love you,

Your youngest son

January 09, 2008

The Power of the Possible

(Columbus, Ga.) Last night I was sitting at the head table at a banquet. The scene is one I have experienced hundreds and hundreds of times.

And a scene, as a young man, I never imagined I would be experiencing.

This past Sunday, I drove over to Sandersville, Ga. to attend a funeral. I did not know until I sat down in the chapel and looked at the memorial folder that my lifelong friend would be doing the eulogy at the funeral.

I was more than impressed by his ability to stand in front of a crowd of folks and communicate what was on his heart concerning his beloved friend. He had the audience leaning on every word and eating out of his hand. In a word, his eulogy was brilliant.

After the service at the cemetery, Jimmy and I walked away from the crowd and had a short conversation. After a few words concerning the reason we were there and my compliments on the great job he did, our discussion turned to the irony that we both ended up speaking in public.

One of our high school teachers has to be turning over in her grave. Or maybe she is turning over in her wheelchair. She may still be alive. We took a speech class together in the tenth grade. Or maybe it was the eleventh. Both of us hated the class and were mortified to stand in front of 25 of our peers and give a three-minute speech. We were terrible at giving speeches. If someone told our teacher in 1971 that Jimmy Childre and Bruce Goddard would be invited to give speeches 38 years later, she would have laughed.

And we would have laughed even more.

There is a lesson here.

What you hate today, may just be what you love tomorrow. What is unthinkable to you today may just be a reality tomorrow.

What you think is impossible today, may just be possible tomorrow.

Never underestimate the power of the possible.

March 17, 2009

A Humbling Thought

My wife and I were in Atlanta today at the Capitol. I actually got to stand at the podium during the morning session of the House of Representatives and make a few comments to the group.

As I suppose you know by now, I have spoken too many times to even think about. But standing in that historic place was a little different. It was so different that I forgot to publicly thank the Speaker of the House for inviting me and Rep. Joe Wilkinson and the others for sponsoring the resolution to bring me there. Not only is that the polite and right thing to do, but it is protocol in the House of Representatives.

So, since I can't do it again there I will do it here:

"Thank you Mr. Speaker for inviting me today and thank you Rep. Wilkinson for sponsoring the resolution presented to me today. And thank you Rep. Katie Dempsey, Rep. Larry O'Neal, Rep. Willie Talton and Rep. Earl Ehrhart for co-sponsoring the resolution."

It really was quite an honor for me, and it was a very special moment for my wife.

My father-in-law, the late Ralph Underwood, was a member of the Georgia House of Representatives some 45 years ago. He died suddenly 35 years ago. My wife was very close to her dad and has many fond memories of being at the Capitol many years ago. This morning she was flooded with memories as she made her first visit back to that floor since she was a little girl and served as a Page. I knew it was a special and even emotional moment for her.

Additionally, my brother-in-law, Rudy (Ralph's only son), handled most of the behind the scenes logistics to get us there. Rudy is a veteran lobbyist and took us around to introduce us to many folks, including a visit with Lt. Governor Casey Cagle in his office. Rudy was in the gallery when Kathy and I were at the podium.

In my short comments, I mentioned my pride of being raised in the community of Reynolds, and I mentioned a couple of the exceptional people who came from there who served at this Capitol. I mentioned a former Lt. Governor of our state, Garland Byrd, and I mentioned my father-in-law, Ralph Underwood.

As I was thinking about what comments I would make this morning, it dawned on me that I had an opportunity of a lifetime not only to be recognized in that historic place but also I had an opportunity to plug the very special community where I was raised. And trust me that community was more than incredible.

I also had the opportunity to remember and honor my wife's dad and my children's granddad. My children never got to meet this granddad. And since they have watched the video of the session this morning, we are already getting more questions from them about their Grandfather Ralph and his public service to the State of Georgia.

I am aware that it has been over 45 years since Ralph Underwood was on the floor of the House of Representatives in our Capitol in Atlanta.

But in some strange way, I had a strong feeling he was there today.

And that is a humbling thought.

April 10, 2007

A Large Slice

When local farmer and picture taker Sidney Bryan placed the photo he took of Buster Byrd in his album in 1978, he wrote these words under it:

"Buster works hard during peanut season and plays hard out of season. Life is a piece of cake and I think Buster will get a large slice."

I think Sidney was not only a farmer, but he might have been a prophet as well.

If I remember birthdays correctly, Buster would have been about to turn 28 years old when Sidney took that picture and placed it in his album. At that time, Buster made his living as a peanut farmer and running a family farm service business.

I spent more than a few nights at the Byrd home when I was growing up. Buster, being four years older than his little brother Chuck and me, didn't cut us much slack during our formative years. Big brothers have a way of doing that to little brothers and their friends.

But I have noticed two things about Buster in the 54 years I've known him:

He loves to have fun, doesn't have many enemies and he lives life on the edge.

Okay I guess that's three things.

But it's a pretty doggoned positive three things.

I don't think I have ever run into Buster when he didn't have a joke to tell or some funny story from days gone by. If the residents of Taylor County, Ga. have 300 nicknames, Buster made up 275 of them. When I was a little kid, he started calling me Lucy. Everybody in town called me that for years. Buster never calls anybody by their real name but rather by their "Buster" name… and yes he still calls me Lucy.

Buster is also somewhat of a musician. Because of his frequent trips to Panama City Beach Florida, many years ago he wrote a song called "Panama City Nights." A recording artist picked it up, and it became a very popular song played on radio stations in Panama City – and radio stations all over for that matter. Buster formed a band and his group became a headliner at the local PC Beach night spots, riding the popularity wave of his hit song.

A man who understands clearly that in order to win, you cannot be afraid to lose; Buster has now become a large land owner in many states and has done very well for himself and his family. As Sidney predicted, Buster did get a large slice of the cake.

For the record, Buster not only has a beautiful wife but he also has four knockout daughters. I happen to know and hug on all of them every time I see them, and I can tell you … they love their daddy.

For Buster, life has always been a piece of cake. And he did get the large slice.

But make no mistake; the ingredients that make that cake taste so good to Buster are those five gals he calls his own.

January 07, 2009

Some Things You Never Forget

Dear Daddy,

It dawned on me yesterday driving down the road that when you were the age I am now, I was playing high school basketball.

You really wanted me to be good at basketball because you paid one of the guys at the store that summer to go with me to the gym after work to throw basketballs back to me every afternoon as I shot until I got blisters on my hand.

You always insisted I could do anything I set my mind to do. Even if it was to play basketball with other guys who were much stronger and much more athletic than me. But you always made sure I knew I could only achieve what I set my mind to achieve if I wanted it bad enough to work hard enough to get it.

It dawned on me many years ago that the lesson you were teaching me as I went to the gym day after day really was much more about life than it was about basketball.

I think you know this by now but just in case you don't - I really did get it. I learned that lesson.

I also remember watching you deal with people. I know you received a degree in Psychology at your beloved Emory, and you were always proud of that. Maybe you learned your people skills from there. I kind of doubt it, but I guess that could be true. But I watched you build enduring relationships with an awful lot of folks. You were never afraid to look someone in the eye and you were never afraid to give someone a hug or a kiss on the cheek when they needed it or maybe you needed it. You always lived on the edge. It was not difficult for you to tell others that you loved them.

And it was also easy for you to say "I'm sorry."

I also remember the loyalty and strong friendships you were determined to continue with your friends from your childhood. When your old friend Ches Marshall came to town, you always hugged him. When one of your childhood classmates died after you retired you cut short your vacation and drove 300 miles to get back to the graveside funeral. It did not matter that you had not seen your friend in 30 years. The fact was he was your friend. You organized an annual gathering of your fraternity brothers just so you could stay in touch with those people of whom you thought so much. I remember the close relationships you had with your lifelong neighbors. Julian Whatley knew as much about your business as any of your family, and Ed Whatley next door was not only your friend and doctor but he was also your confidant. I have a feeling when you died a piece of them died with you. You were that close.

The point is you taught me the value of true friendships. I just want you to know I got that one too. I really did learn that lesson. I don't come close to doing it the way you did it but I understand the truth really well.

I work at keeping those old relationships in my own life alive, because I saw you do it. I have also been fortunate enough to develop a few new ones along the way.

You also spent a lot of time carrying on foolishness. You were always playing a joke on someone or being good natured about the joke someone was playing on you. Though you were a giant of a man and could be very intimidating, you made others at ease around you. You loved to laugh, and you loved to make others laugh. How could I ever forget the time you had a medical procedure scheduled, and you had orders to give yourself an enema the night before? Everybody in the neighborhood showed up for an "Enema Party" with things like Crisco oil and water hoses to help you out. Or the time you were taking up the offering at church and walked with the other three guys up the aisle in front of God and everybody with your offering plate turned upside downwards. Although I think you put the money you collected in another usher's plate, you made it look like that you had collected nothing. I remember you added a lot that day to what I remember as a pretty boring Sunday church service.

I know I cut up way too much. But I got it from you, and I really never spent much time apologizing for seeing the lighter side.

I also remember what you taught me in the business world about integrity and doing the right thing. I always wondered what you could have accomplished in the funeral business if you were in a bigger city. You were absolutely the best at what you did. I also remember that the joking stopped at the door of the funeral home. It was all business there, and I saw up close and personal the compassion you had for people at the absolute worst times in their lives. You were amazing to watch, and I learned more than you ever thought I was learning.

You were at your best when those entrusted to you were at their worst.

I look back on my life when you were here, and I really don't have many regrets. I said and did some stupid things along the way as most kids do. You understood I was growing and you gave me room to grow.

But you also gave me wings to fly.

By the way, if you were still here you would be celebrating your 89th birthday today. At 89, you could probably still beat me in golf.

I guess I just wanted you to know I haven't forgotten.

Some things you never forget.

February 7, 2009

A Gentleman's Game

I played in a golf tournament today with my boss and a few colleagues. Since I hardly have time to play golf anymore, and there was no telling how I would play, I was not even sure if I would enjoy it. It turned out to be a great day and great fellowship with some great folks.

Some of the best memories I have in life were made on the golf course. Although Reynolds was a very small town we were fortunate enough to have a golf course. And I spent many hours on the Reynolds Kiwanis Golf Course as a young boy. Before I was old enough to drive, my mama would drop us off at the golf course early on Saturday morning and pick us up at sundown. It was not unusual for us to play 63 holes of golf in a day. When baseball was not in season there was nothing else to do in Reynolds.

Not only did I learn to appreciate the game, I learned a few life lessons in the process. Golf is a gentlemen's game, and golf etiquette can also be applied to life.

For instance, I learned to never hit out of turn. I learned to be quiet and still when someone else was addressing the ball. I learned never to walk in someone's line. I learned to never criticize someone's futile attempt and always compliment the other's great effort. I learned to repair all divots, fix all ball marks and rake all traps. I learned to let others play through who are playing faster than your group. I learned to count all my strokes and never improve my lie when no one is watching. I learned I did not need an umpire or a referee but my integrity was enough. I learned never to hit when there is danger of hitting someone else. In case that happens accidentally, I learned to yell "fore" to warn the person who is in danger of getting hit.

In this thing we call life, we all could use a little etiquette. By the way, etiquette is basically a discipline of being considerate of others.

In life, we always should know when it is our turn to act or react. In other words, we should know when to speak and when to shut up. We should know when to move and when to be still. We need to pay attention to what others are saying or doing and never get in their way in the process. We should be very slow to criticize and very quick to compliment a great effort. We should always clean up behind ourselves to make life better for those who will follow. We should pace ourselves but never get in the way of someone who is quicker and better. We should always live so one will never have to question our integrity. And contrary to popular opinion, we don't have to destroy someone else to be successful.

Golf is definitely a gentleman's game. It would not be fun if it was played any other way.

And we would all do ourselves a great favor if we apply the same discipline and etiquette to our lives.

May 21, 2007

One Very Special Weekend

When I was growing up I was always surrounded by Whatleys. They lived next door, they lived across the street and they lived down the street.

Whatleys were everywhere.

Julian and Sue Whatley lived across the street. They were the ones with the swimming pool and when they built that pool their backyard became the neighborhood hangout. And I have a lot of testosterone charged memories of summer afternoons at their pool. I usually made sure I was in charge of making sure all the girls had their suntan lotion rubbed on really well. But the Goddard boys were hanging out at that house way before they built their pool. Julian and Sue were very close friends with my mom and dad. Their daughters, Debbie and Donna, are like our sisters, and Julian and Sue are like our second parents.

Those kinds of relationships only happen over a long period of time. I call them cumulative relationships. A lot of unforgettable small moments that together eventually become long lasting memories that become a big part of who you are today. You know exactly what I am taking about.

This weekend I was reminded of a few of those moments. Julian and Sue joined the entire Goddard family in the North Carolina Mountains this weekend. And we had plenty of time to talk, laugh and remember as we sat on the front porch overlooking the Great Smoky Mountains. Julian made a comment on the way home this afternoon and I quote, "One great thing about going off with the Goddards is you never have to worry about trying to think of what to say. The conversations flow freely."

And so do the stories. And so do the laughs. And so do the memories.

Many moons ago our two families vacationed together and camped at a campground about 15 minutes from where we were staying this weekend. We decided to ride over and check it out. After much discussion, we figured that we camped there first in 1965, which would be 42 years ago. In an amazing journey back in time, we found the campground and identified exactly the spot where we parked our camper. We saw the lake where we fished, the lake where we swam and the creek where we played as kids. We even visited with the campground owner Betty, who along with her husband Tom, ran this campground when we were there 42 years ago. She told us Tom left one morning 32 years ago and never returned. Maybe he found greener pastures with a younger woman at another campground. Betty is not sure what happened. I am not sure either.

But what I am sure of is lifelong friendships like we have with the Whatleys are worth far more than silver or gold. I am also sure I was born at the perfect time in the perfect place and into a wonderful family, and people like Julian and Sue Whatley were a major part of it all.

This was absolutely one very special weekend. One the children of Ed and Naia Goddard will always remember.

July 01, 2007

30 Years and Counting

In 1977, Jimmy Carter became President of the United States, Elvis Presley was found dead in his bathroom at Graceland and "Three's Company" debuted on television.

And I got married for the first time. And the only time. In fact, exactly 30 years ago today Kathy Underwood became Kathy Goddard. We had no idea what we were getting into but three grown boys, two daughters-in-law and a 5 month old grandbaby later, it has been quite a journey.

How does one survive 30 years of marriage?

I think at least part of the answer to that question lies in the person you choose to marry. I quickly found that I could not argue when the person with whom I was trying to argue would not argue. I could not fight when the person I was trying to fight refused to fight. By the way that principle is straight out of the Good Book. "A gentle answer turns back wrath but a harsh word stirs up anger" (*Prov* 15:1 NIV). The person I married has always had a special way of delivering a gentle answer. And I just don't remember many harsh words coming out of her mouth in the last 30 years.

I also learned that there has to be more than a little grace extended along the way. If my wife had expectations of having a perfect husband, she quickly realized I did not come close to living up to those expectations. But she extended grace (unmerited favor) in spite of my shortcomings. She set me free to be the imperfect person I was and in giving that freedom I think she got a much better husband.

But I think the greatest secret we have learned in surviving 30 years of marriage is in the area of forgiveness. We have a hard fast rule at our house. If we have a disagreement today we NEVER EVER bring up a shortcoming of the past. That is absolutely below the belt, and we just don't do it.

Years ago I saw a movie called "Indecent Proposal." There was a quote in that movie that I never forgot that was something like this: "If two people love each other they do things to each other. And if they stay together it is not because they forget but it is because they forgive."

Extending grace and forgiveness is not just a spiritual concept but it is simply a choice we make. If we understand the grace and forgiveness that has been extended to us from above, it is only natural that we extend the same to grace to people in our lives. Especially to the people we have chosen to spend our entire lives with.

For the past 30 years, I have been the recipient of an unbelievable amount of grace. Not only from the God of our universe but also from my wife.

And I think that is why we are now at 30 years and counting.

July 03, 2007

The Way We Handle the Moment

(Warner Robins, Ga.) It was a rainy day in Georgia today. There were tears along with the rain. Events honoring twelve-year-old boys will do that to you.

The first event was a parade and a thundering rally held in the civic center here honoring a group of twelve-year-old kids who just brought home a world championship to this middle Georgia town. As my wife and I sat among a large crowd of supporters today, I fought tears and shed others as I watched the videos and listened to the speeches honoring this remarkable group of kids. They went to Williamsport to play a game. In the end they were winners of the game but in winning the game they gave the whole world a lesson about life we won't forget any time soon. In an incredible act of sportsmanship as the whole world watched, these 12-year-old boys suddenly stopped their celebration to console the devastated Japanese boys who had just lost the game.

I learned we all can learn a lot from twelve-year-old kids. And although I really know none of these kids personally, I felt the need to take a few hours on this Saturday to participate in the celebration that was held to honor them.

I came home from that very emotional event to change clothes and head to another very emotional event at my church that was being held in honor of another twelve-year-old boy. I had never met this kid either, but I felt the urge to attend his funeral. I shed more tears as I listened to a heart broken dad talk about his beloved son and incredibly thank God he had him for 12 years . . . instead of 12 days . . . or even 12 hours.

I was reminded again today that life really is a journey that is made up of moments. Sometimes the moment can be so exhilarating you can hardly grasp it. Other times the moment can be so painful you can hardly get your breath.

I was also reminded that it is not the moment that defines us. But it is the way we handle the moment. I saw champions on both ends of the spectrum today. I was moved to tears by both.

September 01, 2007

Chicken George

I have never attended anything like it. Not even close. People literally came from all across the country to play in it. It was THE happening in Reynolds every summer for more than a decade.

The ***Chicken George Invitational Golf Tournament*** was founded, directed and produced by none other than my brother, Chicken George himself.

George was born on April 12, 1952 at Sams-Whatley Hospital in Reynolds, the day after and in the same place as one of his grade school classmates, Gary Parks. He always wondered if Mama brought the wrong baby home from the hospital.

The Chicken George Tournament began small as a gathering of Lambda Chi fraternity brothers from the University of Georgia, but it grew into much more.

As many as 150 golfers, and I use the term "golfers" loosely, played in a two day, 36 hole tournament on the 9 hole golf course in Reynolds. Counting the golfers and their families, Reynolds would easily increase its population by 50 percent during that weekend.

Most of the out of town golfers and their families stayed with locals at their homes in Reynolds or Butler or somewhere in between. Most stayed at the same house year after year because they became friends with their hosts. It was a great deal. Nice accommodations, great breakfast in the mornings. At no cost to the consumer.

The weekend usually kicked off on Friday at noon when Chicken George would arrive in town and do the Kiwanis Club program. Many times he would bring his college buddy, Big Denny, with him, and they would entertain the local Kiwanis crowd with a little guitar picking. They would sing such original songs as, "Slow Drip Coffeemaker" and "Elsie Moo Love" from their popular album, *Big Denny and Chicken George Live in Woodstock with Moo Love.* Some songs they would make up as they went along.

The golfers would start coming in on Friday afternoon and most would try to get in a practice round after the gnats starting calming down late in the day. You could feel the excitement building all over Reynolds. Business also picked up for the local merchants, especially at Johnny Crooks Gas Station. Johnny told me he sold more beer during the Chicken George weekend than he did all the other weekends in a year – added together.

Mama and Daddy's house was always full of golfers and their families and most of the other golfers not staying there would stop by at some point during the weekend and Mama (Chicken Naia) would give them the plan of salvation.

So business picked up for Johnny Crook and Mama during the Chicken George weekend.

For many of the golfers, the first time they played golf was at a Chicken George, and for many others it would be the only time they played all year. But there were some very good golfers who played year after year. Many times there would be a playoff late on Sunday afternoon to determine the champions. There would be a huge gallery following the golfers in the playoff, and all the gallery would be riding in gas golf carts.

During the playoffs, you could hear a pin drop when the golfers were addressing a ball or leaning over a putt. Then you would hear all the gas golf carts cranking up and heading to the next shot. It was a sight to behold.

The galleries at Augusta National had nothing on the galleries at the Chicken George.

A golf pro from St. Simons sent a letter to George one year, and said he came back year after year because it was golf in its purest form.

Not sure about golf's purest form … but it sure was golf in its most fun form.

Some interesting things happened during the Chicken George. The president of the Women's Missionary Society from the church almost fainted one Saturday afternoon when she was walking past the swimming pool. She was flashed by a golfer's girlfriend--a girl gone wild. Reynolds was not quite ready for that.

And Ed Cooper, the manager of the golf club, got really upset when someone went out to the course in the middle of the night and sawed down a huge tree in front of number seven tee. A golfer's ball had apparently hit that tree earlier that day, and he didn't want to have to deal with it on the Sunday round.

When the rumors started flying that Larry Fuller and Bryant Wynn teed off number eight naked as a couple of jaybirds, Chicken George decided he better start making some rules.

He ended up with two: 1) Please keep your clothes on at all times during play on the golf course, and 2) No dancing on the golf course.

Chicken George finally got married and settled down. And the tournament got too big and people got too serious – so he finally ended it.

Crooks Service Station went out of business and Mama started a ministry to the old ladies in town. Everything worked out and life went on.

But Chicken George still wonders if he really belongs to Ted and Mattie Parks.

August 11, 2006

You Might Just Find a Way to Miss It

(Meridian, Miss.) Being a certified road warrior, I eat in more restaurants than you can shake a stick at. If chain restaurants such as Longhorn's, Outback, Red Lobster and all the others gave frequent eater miles, I would have definitely earned a few trips by now.

But I have learned if I really want to find the best eating places, I need to ask the locals. At lunch, we ate at a little hole in the wall diner called "News." I was reminded of my youth eating Sunday dinner at ML and Daisy's restaurant in Reynolds. Today it was the best country fried steak, fresh vegetables, great sweet tea and homemade coconut pie. As wonderful as the food was, the conversation I overheard from three retired men at the next table was probably just as good. They were discussing such things as the speed of a fastball of a pitcher they knew when they were youngsters playing baseball. It's just something special about the simple living in the Deep South. When we were paying the bill, I couldn't help but notice the photos framed on the wall of singer/dancer/movie star Patrick Swayze. Of course I asked and the owner told me he stopped in a few years ago for lunch. I couldn't help but smile.

And I gained a little respect for Patrick.

Tonight, we hit gold at a fine dining establishment called 'Rustlers." It sits right next to a mobile home park, and we literally parked within 10 feet of rather dilapidated single wide mobile home. Since the door of the mobile home was open and we could not help but see in the windows and open door, we got a rather first hand view of this family's Tuesday evening as we got out of our car. Not knowing what to expect when I walked into the restaurant, I was shocked at the dim lights, soft music, real table cloths and tuxedo clad waiters. The service was as good as I have ever seen, and the steak was as good as I have ever had anywhere. I have eaten more than a few.

The lesson here is if you want to find the best life has to offer, sometimes you have to get off the main road and take a chance. If you really want to know the answer to your question, it's a good thing to ask the people who really know.

This is an amazing country. But if you stay on the road everybody else is traveling, you might just find a way to miss it

February 05, 2008

Highest Calling

I have been to a ton of funeral services and memorial services in my life. I thought I had seen it all. But I have never been to a service that compares to the one I attended today.

I got notification last week that they were having a memorial service for Ephraim Johnson at Central State Hospital today, although I had attended his funeral a few days earlier. As his legal guardian, I suppose I am considered his only survivor. Although I feel strongly that I have carried out the wishes of both my dad and Ephraim's mother, I felt compelled to go to this service today.

I'm glad I did.

The audience was made up largely of elderly people who have been life-long residents of this state mental hospital. To put it lightly, when I stood up to say a few words to this group, I saw one of the saddest sights I've ever seen. I couldn't help but wonder how many of the residents have families that even check on them. I would think that the most were put there many years ago when they were young and now their parents have died. Maybe some have relatives who have forgotten. I'm sure that is not true for all, but I would bet that is true for most. It was obvious that they were severely mentally handicapped. I can tell you it was difficult for me to keep my train of thought when trying to communicate with this audience.

But as I was feeling sorry for the residents, I was inspired by the caregivers sitting by their sides. I'm not sure how many patients per caregiver there were, but the ratio was very small. In other words there were a lot of caregivers. I could not help but think about the special person it takes to spend their days caring for someone severely mentally challenged. It has to be a calling.

I am convinced God did not put these mentally challenged folks on earth for themselves. I feel certain He put them here for us--to give all of us an opportunity to show compassion for people who cannot take care of themselves.

Success is not about how much money we make or our position in life or what we have accumulated. But success is about using our God-given talents to help people God has put in our paths.

I saw that as clearly as I've ever seen it today.

It is the highest calling we have.

March 26, 2008

A Very Good Thing

At this church, they really do come "Just as I Am," - just as the old traditional hymn says. Since our oldest son and his bride attend North Point Community Church regularly, we visited today. I think this is our third visit. My eyes get opened a little wider on each visit.

They come in droves on Sundays to this church. There is no telling how many volunteers are working traffic, parking lots, greeting folks, working information desks, book stores and teaching children. It is phenomenal just to watch.

They have three adult worship services each Sunday. They come wearing flip flops and shorts and pony tails - sort of how you would show up at the mall on a Saturday morning. You couldn't find a necktie on a man in this group if your life depended on it.

There is no Sunday School but there are ministries for kids with such names as Wuamba Land, Upstreet, Kidstuff, Xtreme and Inside Out. There are approximately 5,000 kids participating every Sunday at the three campuses—Alpharetta, Cumming, and Buckhead. When you add the 17,000 adults (and growing) in attendance each Sunday, you can't help but think they are doing something very right.

Just for information, this church was started by Andy Stanley 13 years ago. In addition to all the volunteers, they now have 300 full time staff members.

Andy started this church on the premise that Atlanta did not need another church. "What Atlanta does need," he said, "is a safe environment where the unchurched can come and hear the life-changing truth that Jesus Christ cares for them and died for their sin."

Although the message communicated here is biblical and solid as a rock, interestingly some religious people don't like it and others find something to complain about. They complain about such things as the contemporary and loud music, the lighting, the fact they don't have Sunday school and the fact that people wear flip flops and shorts to church, and the fact that they don't give altar calls at the end of the service. So those folks find somewhere else to go to church that better suits their fancy.

I get the feeling that this church is filled with folks whose lives are in shambles, whose marriage has fallen apart, whose business has failed or who have made a ton of money and have figured out that money does not bring happiness.

As Andy said this morning, he never wants this church to be an "ought to" church, where people attend out of duty. I wonder if the "ought to" churches are those we have to dress up outwardly and inwardly to attend.

But they come to this church wearing their flip flops and shorts and shortcomings and brokenness and weaknesses, and they come because they want to come.

I am confident that many reading this do not like even the idea of what this church and churches like it are doing. There is nothing wrong with feeling that. I can understand it feels respectful to dress up on Sunday morning to go to church – I've done it most of my life. The truth is if you feel you need to dress up to go to church, you would not feel comfortable at North Point.

But from North Point's vantage point, that is probably a very good thing.

That just leaves more room at their church for people who are not dressing up to come to yours.

August 10, 2008

You Never Know

Sometimes you just need to get the cobwebs out. It has to be a good thing when two men who started life together and grew up together get away from the rat race of the pressure of running businesses and making decisions and giving speeches to relax and catch up on 36 years of living.

We were born 54 years ago in 1954 and only 17 days apart. When we were babies our mamas had us christened on the same Sunday morning. We played little league baseball together and spent the night in each other's homes too many times to count. We rode together to high school almost every single day after we were old enough to drive.

The truth is I don't have many memories growing up that do not include Jimmy Childre, Jr. Although in many ways our lives have taken different paths for the past 36 years, we have reminded each other of our lifelong friendship every year since we became adults. Every September 3rd, Jimmy gets a call from me to wish him a Happy Birthday. Every September 20th, I get a call from him.

We forget a lot of stuff, but neither of us forgets to make that call.

This year we decided we would do more than give each other a call. To celebrate our upcoming birthdays, we decided to take a road trip. And that's why tonight I find myself writing from the heart of New York City. It's hard to believe one can come to New York City, the rat race capital of the world, to get away from the rat race.

But trust me we did.

The last two days, under the auspices of leisurely sightseeing, we have laughed way too much but have also discussed every subject under the sun. Besides attending a game at old Yankee Stadium, which was the real excuse for the trip, we have had some rather long meals where the conversation went from childhood memories to politics to theology to education to life stories to frivolous discussions.

We spent about an hour in the fabulous Waldorf Astoria Hotel yesterday morning and were reminded of the history of that great hotel and people who have stayed there. Afterwards we spent another hour at the Mercedes Dealership on Park Avenue which was designed by Frank Lloyd Wright, the most prolific and influential architect of the 20th century. Amazingly we discovered they deliver about 150 new Mercedes per month at this store. We also found out they sell about 25 Maybachs per year, which I couldn't help but notice listed for about $370K.

We spent about two and a half hours having lunch at the Boathouse Restaurant overlooking the lake in Central Park. I can't think of many places where the atmosphere could be better for conversation. We had dinner the night before at the famous Tavern on the Green. Tonight, after a Broadway show, we ended up in the old Paramount Theater which is now the Hard Rock Café and had late night burgers and enjoyed the rock and roll history and memorabilia of NYC.

There were no schedules to keep and no place to be at a certain time. But we now are about to head back to where there are schedules to keep and places we have to be at certain times.

Neither of us is complaining.

Jimmy and I grew up together, went our separate ways, and met in NYC for an evaluation. We both agreed in some areas we got it right and some areas we got it wrong. But hopefully we both have a lot of living to do before we get to the end of the journey.

But you never know.

Here's hoping we meet here again when we are 80 so we can discuss how it all turned out.

August 19, 2008

College Football Heaven

(Athens, Ga.) There is nothing like being in Athens and "Between the Hedges" on a Saturday afternoon. That is especially true when it is opening day, and your team begins the season ranked Number One in the nation. It just doesn't get better… unless your team keeps winning and ends the season ranked Number One. Then it really doesn't get better.

As is true on most major college campuses around the country, the happening is as much about what goes on outside the stadium as the game itself. I was reminded of that as we drove into Athens on Saturday morning. It took us two and a half hours to drive (if you call it driving) the 30 miles or so from Madison to Athens. I figured out quickly that there are a ton of other folks who believe there is nothing better than being in Athens for the opening day of football season. I also realized that there would be as many people outside the stadium as would be inside.

Yesterday, I couldn't help but think about how things have changed since I first arrived here as a college freshman 36 years ago.

For starters, the girls are much cuter and younger than they were 36 years ago. Maybe it's because I am a lot older and uglier than I was 36 years ago, but when I visit with old college friends' children who were only a twinkle in my friends' eye when I was in school, I definitely feel old. Sarah Tippins is the daughter of a couple of my college friends. Sarah is a senior at UGA and is not only cute as a button but has personality to boot. She was tailgating with her parents and other friends when we crashed their party. My mama used to tell me that young folks who make older folks feel special are special folks themselves. I think I understood that principle better than ever after visiting with this sweetheart yesterday.

Speaking of tailgating, when I was in school it was really was tailgating. Parents would pull up in their station wagons and open the tailgate and use it for a table for their Kentucky Fried Chicken and Pimento Cheese sandwiches before going in the stadium. Now there are elaborate tents and tent communities with home team logos, adult beverages, grills on wheels with the aroma of grilled chicken and steaks and ribs in the air, with many of the folks not having any intention of actually going to the game. You must know that the stadium holds only 93,000 folks, so there is no way all these folks could even begin to fit in the stadium.

And speaking of fitting in the stadium, tickets are also a little more difficult to come by than they were in 1972. In 2008, if you are not a season ticketholder, you have to donate a measly $10,000 to the Athletic Association for the privilege of purchasing two season tickets in the nose bleed section. The donation minimum goes up every year. That may explain why there are as many people outside the stadium as inside.

My wife and her sister were part of the crowd who did not attend the game yesterday. They decided to spend the afternoon in downtown Athens shopping. They proved my point when they said that there were waits of over an hour to get in the restaurants during the game. When I was in school, Athens was a ghost town while the game was going on.

I also couldn't help but see some young folks get escorted out of the stadium by the GBI during the game. I did not notice any bad behavior, so I figured Big Brother must have been watching carefully for underage drinking. When I was in school you would have to get into a drunken fist fight, throw your drink in an officer's face, and moon the guy you were fighting to get escorted out of the stadium.

Some things have definitely changed. But there is one thing that has not changed.

Athens Georgia is still college football heaven. And if you folks out there who are not believers say your prayers at night and live right, you might make it there one fall Saturday afternoon.

August 31, 2008

The Big Streak of '74

This is a story that needs to be told. You are about to read an eyewitness account of the biggest streak in the history of the United States. It happened in the spring of 1974 in Athens, Georgia. I was there. Saw it all. And all saw me.

My daddy was paying a lot of money for me to get an education. I was getting more of an education than he realized. A buddy and I were riding along in my 1964 push button Plymouth listening to the tunes from WRFC AM radio station. All of a sudden the announcer on the radio interrupted the music and said that the station had just received a call that a sorority was about to streak in front of their radio station.

We looked at each other and did what any other warm blooded 19 year old boys would do. We made a U-Turn and headed to the radio station. I think every other UGA student in Athens heard that announcement and did the same thing. There was a major traffic jam in front of the radio station by the time we got there.

The longer we waited – the bigger the crowd got. Everybody was waiting for a truckload of naked girls to arrive on the scene. After a couple of hours, we decided it had to be a hoax. Then all of a sudden a truck pulled up and about 12 naked guys jumped out of the back of the truck. The girls in the crowd screamed and scattered.

It was the funniest thing I had ever seen in my life.

Later that same night we heard a crowd was gathering in front of one of the large girls dorms. We headed there and found quite a show in progress. A light would blink off and on in a certain room to get everybody's attention. And then the light would come on for about 5 seconds and a naked girl would appear in the window. This went on for hours with many girls as participants.

Somewhere in South Georgia a couple of proud parents sitting in their den thought their innocent little girl was in a library somewhere studying.

The next afternoon from the front porch of the LXA house we watched as some girls from a nearby sorority exposed their booties in the car windows for us as they rode by.

It wasn't long before every guy I knew was taking his clothes off--big people, little people, fat people, skinny people. It didn't matter. Athens became the naked city.

Every night that week was like Mardi Gras. There was a continuous parade of cars and trucks honking their horns with naked people on the hoods or trunks or in the back of the trucks riding down Milledge Avenue. And there were large crowds on both sides of the road cheering them on all the way.

The news media came in from all over and one of my fraternity brothers who was on the gymnastics team got himself on the 6:00 p.m. news in Atlanta. His parents called the fraternity house looking for him, and they were not happy. They had just seen their athletic son on TV doing flips through the Bulldog Room … buck naked.

We got used to seeing naked people. I remember one late night at the Krystal when I looked up and saw a guy as naked as he came into the world standing in line waiting to give his order. All he had on were his tennis shoes.

The funny thing was that nobody was even paying attention to him.

One night two crazy guys dribbled a basketball down Milledge Avenue and into a sorority house. The ball went under a sofa, and the dribbler got a standing ovation from the girls when he bent down to get it.

Later in the week a group began to pass out flyers to get everybody to participate in the big streak. The organized effort was to set the national record for having the most naked people in one place.

The appointed date and time came. The national media were there. A Lady Godiva was riding her white horse. There were naked people everywhere – cheek to cheek. Gym shorts in hand. The men who liked men were in hog heaven. When some of us realized that, we quietly slipped our gym shorts back on and waited for the running to begin.

Everyone met at Myers quadrangle on South Campus. The plan was for everyone to gather there and be counted and then to run across Sanford Stadium bridge to Reed quadrangle on North Campus.

There were throngs of people on both sides of the path cheering the naked runners on. People had come from miles around to witness the event. Perverted men from places like Winder and Monroe even brought their wife and kids to witness the event.

I'm not sure where they keep such records, but I was told we did set the national record for having the most naked people in one place at one time in the history of the United States.

I'm not sure what I will be known for when my time on earth is done.

But it should be known that I participated in the largest streak in the history of the United States in Athens, Georgia in the spring of 1974.

And I have a scar on my rear end to prove

August 12, 2006

True Blessings

I had one of those rare weeks this past week when I did not travel. It will be the last one of those until the holidays, but I needed the time in the office. I also got to do some things I normally can't do.

For starters we were having a conference at our church that I attended two different nights. It was a pastor's conference that featured excellent speakers who are pastors of some of the largest churches in America. I'm not a pastor but Lord knows I've known a few. I have also buried a few. I figured they could use a little support from a friendly undertaker before their church members kill them.

I also had my annual (or is it called anal) physical this week. I checked out good. I need to exercise more, but I think I'm good for at least another year. I still have to schedule a colonoscopy and hope to get that done before the end of the year. It's all part of growing up I suppose.

After I left the doctor's office, I decided to drop by and vote since I will be out of town on the big day. The "drop by" turned into standing in line for an hour. But it was worth it because I heard the quote of the year as I was standing in the very long line.

A couple of young voters came in with their big caps and wearing their favorite professional football jerseys. When they saw the long line one of the guys happened to be right next to me when he said, *"I don't think I like Obama that much."* He and his buddy left without voting.

This week I also got to spend some quality time with the wife and the family. Kathy and I actually had dinner together every night. I had some great bonus "Taylor" time with our little grandbaby girl. I spent one of the best Saturdays I can remember. All my boys and their ladies were here. At lunch, while the girls were out gallivanting and getting haircuts and such with their mother-in-law, my three boys and I had lunch at a local eatery. Afterwards we came home and cheered the Georgia Bulldogs to victory. By sundown, everybody was under one roof and eating homemade chili and enjoying the moment. Later in the night, I walked upstairs, and there were at least five folks on our bed watching something on TV. If it gets any better than that for a dad, please let me know where it is, and I want to go soon.

Earlier in the week, I stopped by the Children's Hospital at lunch to visit a sweet little baby girl who had been diagnosed with an illness called Kawasaki

Disease. I had never heard of such a disease but whatever it is, little Izzy is now home and doing fine. As you can imagine her mom and dad stayed at the hospital around the clock with their little girl, and mama even slept very uncomfortably in the crib with her.

Is there anything a parent would not do for their children?

For me the answer to that question is easy.

It's about unconditional love. It is the relentless variety. You love them when they are healthy, and you love them when they are sick. You love them when they get it right, and you love them when they get it wrong. You are reminded of all that when everyone is sitting around a table eating a hot bowl of chili on a cool Saturday night.

Thank God for the true blessings of life.

October 26, 2008

Go Sit and Rock and Smoke Your Pipe

The tradition of the pipe between the Goddards and the Whatleys began in 1933. Dr. Clifford and Mary Monk Whatley gave an old corn cob pipe to my grandfather, George Henry Goddard for his 50th birthday.

There was also this message, "Old man go sit and rock and smoke your pipe."

The pipe hung on the wall in my grandfather's office until Mrs. Mary turned 50, and he gave it back to her with the same message. "Old woman go sit and rock and smoke your pipe."

When my grandparents celebrated their 50th wedding anniversary, the pipe came back to them with the same message. When Mrs. Mary turned 70, she got the pipe back. My grandfather received the pipe back on his 90th birthday.

When Ed Whatley (son of Clifford and Mary Whatley) turned fifty years, my grandfather decided it was time to pass the pipe down to the next generation. He gave it to my dad and told him to keep the tradition going. So my dad and mom presented the pipe to Dr. Ed Whatley with the same message, "Old man go sit and rock and smoke your pipe."

The pipe was swapped back and forth on special birthdays and special occasions between the next generation of our two families--always with the same message. "Old man go sit and rock and smoke your pipe."

In July of 2000, Dr. Whatley and Rosemary came out to my house in Reynolds and gave me the pipe. He figured it was time to pass the pipe down to the third generation. He included a note about the history of the pipe and also these words: "This old box, pipe and letters are part of a lot of history of our two families. Keep it going."

When Dr. Whatley's son, Jim, turned 50 years old he got the pipe from me. I included a letter about the history of the pipe. Jim not only turned 50 but he had recently given his oldest daughter in marriage. My words were, "I can't think of a better time to return this pipe. This year you have definitely earned the right to relax a little . . . so old man go sit and rock and smoke your pipe."

When my brother George turned 50, Jim gave the pipe back to him with another personal letter that ended with the same message, "Old man go sit and rock and smoke your pipe."

When I turned 50 a couple of years ago, I got the pipe back from my brother with the same message. Included in his letter were these words:

We all grew up and moved from Reynolds (except for you until later), started our careers and families and moved away from a life-style that created families that were friends for generations. We grew up in the South where our parents were life-long friends with other couples and enjoyed the simple pleasures of each other's company. We all have fond memories of backyard cookouts, fish fries, swimming parties and all of us kids playing together. Not watching TV or playing video games but actually interacting with each other. We all live busy lives but in all of this busyness we should not forget what our years in Reynolds gave us… ROOTS! May the world see this pipe that was first given by Mary Whatley to George Goddard in 1933 and be reminded that we have all strayed too far from home. And it's time to go back!

So the pipe has become a symbol for us not only of the special relationship our families have enjoyed for generations but a symbol of our common roots in a small south Georgia town.

Maybe there is a special message in this special pipe for all of us.

Maybe we all need to slow down and remember our roots.

And spend more time building enduring relationships.

And go sit and rock and smoke our pipe.

September 3, 2006

I Am Thankful

Last week, I was on an elevator in a hotel when a stranger joined me. I spoke to him and asked him how he was doing. He quickly responded, "I'm living the dream." That guy caused me to have a very early morning smile.

I was reminded I'm getting to do the same. I sure am thankful for the opportunity to live it. In fact, I'm thankful for a lot of stuff.

I am thankful for all the struggles. There have been plenty along the way, and I know they will continue to come. But I know I'm always much better off having gone through them than I would be without them.

I'm thankful for Friday nights. During the last couple of years, Friday night has been "Taylor" night at our house. Just the thought of snuggling with my beautiful grandbaby girl can cause me to tear up. She is a true gift from God.

I'm thankful for the power of laughter. I love to laugh and I love to see others laugh. It really is medicine for the soul.

I'm thankful for old friends. Having grown up in a small town where friends are generational, I get to have relationships with folks most can't understand. It is a special thing to run into someone I have known all my life and know their grandparents and most likely the names of their great grandparents. Those guys get a hug from me when I see them. The gals get a kiss.

I'm also thankful for new friends. I have been given the opportunity to meet and build relationships with a lot of folks in different parts of the country. I have decided that people are basically the same wherever they live. There are a few jerks here and there, but most folks are just wonderful if you take time to get to know them.

I'm thankful for memories of the greatest parents a boy could possibly have. Like everybody else, they were not perfect but for some reason all I remember now is the perfect stuff.

I'm thankful for the opportunity that comes my way from time to time to help somebody who is in the ditch of life. It's a blessing when I find myself in the right place at the right time, and I'm thankful for the many folks who have helped me out of the ditch along the way.

I am thankful for my church and the small group we meet with on a regular basis. To these young couples, I am not co-worker or boss or dad or anything. I'm just Bruce, and we are building relationships that will last a lifetime.

I'm thankful that I am gainfully employed. In the world we live in now, that is truly a blessing. You won't find me complaining about long hours or traveling or anything else related to work. I'm just thankful to get to do it.

I am thankful for my siblings and their families and my wife's siblings and their families. Everybody loves each other and is on speaking terms. Before the holiday season is over, both families will gather and celebrate life and the reason for the season.

I am thankful for my three imperfect sons. If they were perfect they would not belong to me. They all are different. They all are gifted. And they all love their mom and dad. What a blessing they are.

I am thankful for my two perfect daughters-in-law and the future perfect daughter-in-law in waiting. When my boys were little, I always wondered who they would marry. These girls have far and away exceeded all my hopes and dreams. I am one blessed daddy-in-law. I take care of them because I'm sure these girls will one day decide which nursing home to put me in.

I am thankful for my wife. This past July, Kathy and I celebrated our 31st anniversary. She puts up with a lot being married to me. She is once, twice, three times a lady. And I love her.

More than anything I'm thankful for an awesome God who has given me purpose in life, and the opportunity to live my dream. Or maybe it's His dream for me.

November 27, 2008

Eulan Brown's Proudest Moment

I spoke Friday at the Kiwanis Club of Taylor County. Since these are home folks I did not really plan anything particular to talk about except I knew I wanted to end my remarks by talking about the lessons of Eulan Brown. Unlike all the other places I have told this story, most of the people in this audience knew Eulan personally. I received this email earlier today from a long time friend. Butch told me some things I never knew about Eulan. If you remember the CB Radio craze of the seventies, this letter will cause you to smile. I sure did.

Bruce,

I enjoyed your Kiwanis program in Reynolds yesterday. I was really glad to hear about the impact that Eulan Brown has made on you. Eulan spent a lot of time hanging out in my TV repair shop. He was truly a good and gentle person. I miss him.

As you remember, back in the mid 70's the CB radio craze hit Reynolds, Ga. I was in the TV repair business during that era and the CB radio craze was a natural progression to my sales and service business.

Eulan wanted a CB radio real bad. Everybody had one. Your dad had one, Your brother Mac had one (Circuit Rider), our barber Wayne Hill (The Clipper) had several, Gene Brunson (The Plow Boy) had CB's, even Dr. Whatley, Dr. Silverman, and Dr. Frank had CB's. There probably wasn't a person in the community that didn't have a CB. I sold hundreds and serviced thousands.

Eulan especially wanted a CB on his bicycle. Eulan's bicycle was his only mode of transportation, but he was always falling down. It didn't seem like a good idea, but I finally gave Eulan a small walkie - talkie to use on his bicycle. We mounted it on his basket with hay bailing wire. As you can imagine, that didn't last long. He wasn't much out of the driveway when he crashed the bike and broke the walkie-talkie.

In addition to selling Grit newspapers, Eulan also cut lawns to make money. I would occasionally have him cut my lawn. Eulan continued to want a CB radio so bad that I paid him for cutting my grass with a used mobile unit though I refused to put it on his bicycle.

Eulan lived in an apartment next to the bank with his mother and a small dog. I gave him a power supply to power the mobile unit, but he still didn't have *an antenna. An antenna was going to cost Eulan $30 or $40. Eulan had no money.*

I cut a long Bamboo reed (fishing pole) from Fickling Mill and wrapped telephone wire around it, cut it to the right wavelength for CB and nailed it to the side of the apartment for Eulan. It saved him some money and got him on the air.

Eulan was so happy. He was now talking to all the CBer's in town. He had pretty good range with it. He could talk to anybody in Reynolds. He talked to The Laundry Man, Lightfoot, Plowboy, The Clipper, Circuit Rider, The Butcher, The Printer, Well Man, Water Boy and lots of others. I even overheard him talking to the Green Machine in Roberta one night. He was a happy CBer.

Eulan had difficulty talking to people face to face. But, on the CB no one could see his deformity and he was much more confident. He was talking to strangers coming thru town and giving directions to places that I had no idea he even knew existed.

As luck would have it, a storm came thru and down came the fishing pole antenna. Having done all I felt I could to help him because I was really busy during that time doing CB and TV repair work, and dealing with Eulan made me no money whatsoever, I really tried to avoid Eulan.

You know Eulan and he was, if anything, persistent. Even to the point of aggravation. One afternoon, mostly to get him out of my hair, I went up to his apartment to look at his broken down fishing pole antenna.

Eulan had removed the telephone wire from the broken fishing pole and wrapped it around his mother's mop handle. It wouldn't work because the wire was wrapped too loosely, his VSWR was off the scale and he still had the mop head on the handle.

However, it gave me an idea. I gave his mother back her good mop, and found 2 old mop handles around the apartment. I used my Amateur Radio Handbook as a rough guide and began to wind wire around the 2 mop handles in a configuration called co-phasing. It's the same principle used on the big 18 wheel trucks where you see an antenna on each mirror. For best results they need to be separated by 9 foot (1/4 wavelengths). With this configuration you can make the antenna system directional by cutting the wire to specific lengths. It gives it more gain in a particular direction. I spent several days, in my spare time, experimenting with different wire lengths, tightness of the coils, etc and finally came up with a really unique antenna system. I called it "Eulan's co-phased mop handles."

I attached one mop handle to each side of Eulan's roof. The improvement was quite amazing. Eulan was now able to talk to CBer's outside of Reynolds. He could talk to people in Roberta, Ft. Valley, Oglethorpe, Butler, Montezuma, Ideal and occasionally in Thomaston and even farther. At this point you couldn't shut him up. He wanted to stay on the air all the time. Imagine Eulan ON THE AIR all the time.

A really funny thing happened. Probably the favorite thing for an avid CBer to do is to talk skip. I won't try to explain it, but it involves talking to other CBer's a long distance away and usually at night. Our local Barber, Wayne Hill (The Clipper) was also an avid CBer. Wayne had a really nice CB station at that time. He had Stack Threes (A really big antenna), with a rotator on a 50 foot tower, powered by a substantial amplifier. Wayne would occasionally talk skip at night.

One morning Wayne called me. He was frantic. He said "You've got to help me with my dadgum CB radio system." Wayne was one of my best friends. I loved him like a brother. Still do - he's gone now.

It seems that Wayne and Eulan were both trying to talk skip to the same distant person late at night on their CB's. The other person could talk to Eulan but not to Wayne. Wayne was very upset. This was an impossible situation.

Wayne said "you don't understand, I've been beat by a dadgum mop handle"

This was probably Eulan Brown's proudest moment.

KGZ 7898 "The Butcher"

Butch Turner, Reynolds, Ga.

May 24, 2008

Conspicuously Absent

"Ryan Richardson didn't blur racial lines – he erased them."

Those were the words of Jerry Walls, pastor of Southside Baptist Church of Warner Robins, Ga., as he eulogized 19 year old Ryan Kimes-Richardson today in one of the most impressive funeral services I've ever attended.

And trust me, I've attended more than a few.

I began to get impressed on Monday evening when my wife and I attended the visitation at the church.

Okay, I was more than impressed. I was blown away.

I was blown away because there was at least a two hour wait in a line to get to Ryan's parents. I was blown away because so many teenagers stood in that two hour line for the opportunity to hug the parents of their obviously beloved friend. I was blown away because I saw so many tears. I was blown away because of the strength of Ryan's heartbroken parents.

I was blown away because about 98 percent of the hundreds of folks who had gathered were Caucasian, and Ryan happens to be an African American.

I couldn't help but wonder where the media was for this one. It seems we hear so much of racial tension and discord, especially in southern places like middle Georgia. I can tell you racial tension was conspicuously absent at the celebration of this young man's life.

There was also not a dry eye among the 1,000 or so folks who were in attendance at the funeral service today.

My friend and pastor Jerry Walls did a masterful job mixing humor with the heaviness of the moment. Ryan lived life to the fullest, and he left many fun memories with all those who knew him and loved him. Jerry also did a masterful job reminding the throngs of teenagers in attendance who were leaning on his every word that none of us are promised our next breath.

On Friday morning, Ryan's mom sent him to mail a package and find a job. Ryan, in his usual jovial way, danced with his mom in the kitchen before he left.

In a few hours, as our pastor so eloquently said today from the pulpit, "Ryan was dancing before Jesus."

Among other scriptures, the pastor quoted *Proverbs* 18:24: "A man that has friends must show himself friendly."

Ryan Kimes-Richardson made a ton of friends in his short 19 years on earth.

Everyone who attended the funeral service was humbled today as we celebrated this extraordinary young man's life. Ryan's presence and the impact he had on all who knew him were evident to all.

But racial lines were conspicuously absent.

February 17, 2009

Basket Three

Winning

"You will never be winner, until you get to the point that you are not afraid to lose . . . In order to be a winner, you have to be willing to get up earlier, leave later, work harder and give everything you've got and more. Even to the point of getting blisters on your hand. Or even to the point of having skinned knees and elbows from falling off a bicycle. Winning does not come without sacrifice."

She Still Gets My Business

In the mid sixties, the women went to the beauty parlor to get their hair "set" about once a week. The ladies who fixed the hair wore smocks over their shirts and usually wore white shoes. The men went to the barber shop. The men got a haircut about once a month, but they visited the barber more often than that so they could hang out with the guys and shoot the bull. Men sure didn't go to beauty parlors to get their haircut.

At least that was true where I grew up until a lady by the name of Willorene took styling hair to the next level.

Willorene was an entrepreneur. If there ever was an entrepreneur in Reynolds, she was it. She remodeled an old building and ended up with a very large upscale hair salon with waiting area and all. Nobody had ever heard of such a thing in the mid sixties when she made that bold move. She may have had the first upscale hair salon in Georgia. If not, I'm sure it was the first in middle Georgia.

Up until then, beauty parlors consisted of small little rooms that smelled like "permanents" and was crammed with chairs and those hair dryers the little ladies pulled down over their heads.

The Beauty Nook, as it was called, was decorated to the nines. I still remember the colors – gold and green. And the good looking girls who worked there dressed alike and wore gold and/or green short culottes. I probably misspelled that word but it was the little short shorts that looked like mini skirts.

Those outfits just killed me.

I never saw one of the applications Willorene used for the girls to apply for a job there. But somewhere it had to be in writing that an applicant had to be very cute to be hired. My goodness there was some gorgeous, sexy gals who worked in that place. It was the kind of place that a young boy with raging hormones liked to hang out, I can tell you that.

But more than that, the Beauty Nook drew customers from all over middle Georgia. People drove as far as 40 miles to get their hair done there and that was unheard of in those days.

The Beauty Nook also styled men's hair before it was stylish. Think about it – why would a guy go sit in a barber shop with a bunch of old guys when he could go to the Beauty Nook and look at all these beautiful girls? Not hard to figure that out.

She sure got my business.

Willorene, the entrepreneur, made a ton of money. In those days she was a woman business person in a man's world. But she outworked the men and made more money than most. They worked long hours usually starting at 5 a.m. on the weekends and worked well into the night. Whatever she made, she earned it.

Kathy Underwood washed hair at the Beauty Nook when I was in high school. It was when she was working there that I started noticing her. The cute girl in the sexy outfit got my attention. I ended up marrying this Beauty Nook girl.

After many years of working herself to death, Willorene finally left the upscale beauty business and went into the financial services business in Atlanta. She has done as well in that field as she did in the styling business.

This weekend she and her husband, Jerry, stopped by our house. I had called her so she could help me get my new grandbaby set up with a mutual fund. This lady entrepreneur reminded me that time and interest and a little money can produce some amazing results.

I have known Willorene all my life. She has definitely earned the right for me to do business with her. It was through her screening of applicants at the Beauty Nook that I found my wife for goodness' sake.

Now little Taylor gets to benefit as well from this lady entrepreneur. If Taylor will leave the little bit of money I invested for her alone for the next 60 years or so, she will be a millionaire.

Willorene was not wearing her gold culottes Saturday.

But she still gets my business.

February 5, 2007

The Lesson Is for All of Us

While Lehman Brothers was preparing to declare bankruptcy, Merrill Lynch was in the process of getting bailed out by Bank of America, and the insurance giant A.I.G. was getting ready to lend itself $20 billion in an attempt to stay afloat in the face of cuts to its debt rating, a legend of a house builder passed away in a little Georgia town.

In my view, the high flying, high rolling Wall Street fat cats could have learned a lesson or two from the house builder from Reynolds.

Neil Hinton, Jr. was a master carpenter who became a master building contractor. At one time all four of his carpenter brothers worked for him. Later his son would become his business partner. I never saw his motto on a sign in front of a house he was building nor did I see it on a sign at the hardware/building supply store he owned and operated. In fact, I never even heard him say it.

But his reputation was known by everybody who knew him. It was fairly simple too.

"If you want your house built right, let Neil do it. If it's the cheapest price you are looking for, go somewhere else."

Neil certainly never overcharged for his services, but he never cut corners when it came to building a house. In fact, he refused to cut corners when it came to building a house.

Interestingly, most of us can't tell a well built house from a shoddily built house when we ride by it. The basic appearance looks pretty much the same. But when you start comparing the foundations, the flooring, the amount of lumber used, the craftsmanship and the detail, you can quickly tell the difference.

I can't help but think about this principle when I think of what's going on with the Lehman Brothers and Merrill Lynchs of the world today. When we looked at them from our glancing perspective, they looked rather formidable. But inside their earnings were not from recurring businesses, but their earnings depended on a combination of huge leverage, huge risk and ridiculously over compensated employees.

And not a lot of lumber.

Their houses are now falling along with their stock prices. It seems they chose selfishness over the long term health of the house they were building.

If we are not careful, we can follow that same path and end up not having enough lumber and craftsmanship and detail in the lives we are building.

I'm not sure how many worldly goods Neil Hinton, Jr. left my lifelong friends Kim and Kay, who are his children. But if they take his lead, and I know they already have, they have something far more valuable than worldly goods.

September 15, 2008

Strong, Tough and Relentless

I have often wondered how many people give up when the reward for hard work is right around the corner. I have a feeling it happens much too often. For the past four years or so, I've had my eye on a young man who has continued to work extremely hard when most would have given up a long time ago.

I first met James Lipfert when he was in the eighth grade. He spent the night with a group of boys at our house. Our youngest son had transferred to Westfield Schools in Perry, Ga., and James was one of the boys in his class who quickly befriended him and made him feel welcome.

During the next few years I watched James become a leader in his class and ultimately his school. I saw his leadership on the baseball field, the track field, the basketball court, the football field and in the classroom. I couldn't help but smile when he ran over people on the football field when he had the ball or when the other team had the ball. He was strong and tough … and relentless.

And he is still strong and tough and relentless.

But off the field he is always the perfect gentleman. I have always been taught that you can judge a man's character by the way he treats others. I pegged James early on as a young man who had been raised incredibly right by his parents.

When James graduated from high school, he had several opportunities to play college football. When you are selected as Player of the Year in your region two years running, rush for over 1,000 yards, and make over 100 tackles as a junior and senior, college recruiters will be knocking on your door. The challenge is when you graduate from a small private school, the opportunities will most likely come from smaller colleges.

I was not surprised when James decided to forego a college football career at a small college to attend Georgia Tech to pursue a Management degree. I was also not surprised when James walked on the Georgia Tech Football team without a scholarship. Further, I was also not surprised when he made the team. James was redshirted his first year and has spent the last four years as a Georgia Tech Yellow Jacket somehow balancing a very tough academic schedule with a very tough athletic schedule.

With limited playing time but a whole lot of long days and body weary practices for the past four years, James continued his relentless spirit. He simply refused to give up or give in. This year, which is his senior year, James was rewarded for his relentless spirit and hard work when he was given a full athletic scholarship at Georgia Tech.

Napoleon Hill was right when he said, "Effort only fully releases its reward after a person refuses to quit."

James, a young man of great faith, is quick to tell anyone who will listen that he considers himself blessed by God because he was raised by devoted parents, surrounded by fabulous family and friends and raised in a church where he was taught the principles of God's word at an early age.

I have to tell you, this Georgia Bulldog will be looking for #30 every time Georgia Tech takes the field this year, and I will be cheering James Lipfert on every play. More importantly, I will be cheering him on in life after he graduates next year.

Trust me – this strong, tough and relentless gentleman will accomplish great things before he is done.

August 26, 2008

Living to Win

(Jackson, Tenn.) I met a very interesting young lady at the Spaghetti Store tonight in this west Tennessee town. It's always amazing what you can find out about folks if you just start a conversation and ask a question or two... or three.

I am always impressed with young folks who wait on tables. You will usually find that they are either working their way through school or working a part-time job to help their parents out. Either of those scenarios is very honorable. They have figured out that the world owes them nothing and have decided they have to earn their way.

Lori is 22 years of age. She works two jobs and has finished two years of college at Jackson State. By day, she is a pharmacy technician at a local Walgreens. At night, she works as a waitress at the Spaghetti Store. She also happens to be an active member of Englewood Baptist Church in Jackson.

And unlike most 22 year olds, she has saved her money.

In fact, when she was 20 years old she bought a house, and she did it on her own without help from her parents. She said the house is a modest one with one bedroom. But she has just finished redecorating it. To be honest, I don't know many (any) 20 year old girls who buy houses on their own.

I asked one of her co-workers if she could say two things that described Lori, what would she say? She quickly replied, "She is a workaholic, and she sleeps with a shotgun."

Lori made me feel better when she told me the shotgun is actually behind the door. I didn't ask, but I got the impression she knows how to use it.

I also got the impression that one of these days; Lori will have a lot of folks answering to her. As I have said here several times before, most people live every day just to get by. A few folks live to win.

This Lori is living to win.

May 29, 2008

Go War Eagles!

I first met Wendy Willis when she was a young teenager visiting us in Reynolds. I don't remember getting a really good look at her at first because she was always turning flips in the front yard.

The Willis family got the rug pulled out from under them not long after Wendy's first visit to Reynolds. Their dad (and husband) was diagnosed with a fast growing brain cancer.

Before they knew it he was gone.

Doggone it. Life can be tough. This very close knit family had its collective heart ripped apart.

As I have seen replayed time and time again in too many families to count, Elizabeth (the mom) all of a sudden was not just mom but she had to be mom and dad to her three children.

And she did an amazing job.

All three children attended Auburn University and became bona fide War Eagles (bless their hearts). The two oldest, Wendy and Kim, have both graduated and are married. Paul is currently a senior at Auburn.

I don't know why they had to go through what they had to go through. But I do know this: Their dad would be extremely proud of his children.

He would also be extremely proud of his wife.

We know the Willis family because they are neighbors and best friends with some of our family members in Rome, Ga. We spent a lot of time with the Willis over the years. We have been on several beach trips with them and visit every chance we get and just consider them family.

This family is not just "wedding guest" friends. They are "rehearsal dinner" friends. Some of you understand that but if not, the rehearsal dinner list is much shorter than the wedding guest list.

On one of our beach trips years ago, Wendy was very stressed because she was about to go through cheerleader tryouts at Auburn. Not surprisingly, she became an Auburn cheerleader. The next year, I was in a store and picked up a national sports magazine and saw her picture in it. I smiled. Wendy had hit the big time.

We started watching every Auburn football game that came on television, so we could see Wendy cheering on national TV. We had Wendy parties at our house. Not everybody can get a die-hard Georgia Bulldog fan to watch

Auburn football on a regular basis.

Not only was Wendy a cheerleader, but she was also active in a local church in Auburn. She met a wonderful guy at that church who would eventually become her husband. Kevin and Wendy felt a calling on their lives and for a couple of years they have been preparing to do what they are doing now.

They have dedicated their lives to their calling and have recently moved on the other side of the world. Their plan is to be there at least for three years.

We got an email from Wendy yesterday. The communication is cryptic in nature because of the condition in which they live in the Pacific Rim. All communication is monitored.

Hey Uncle Bruce and Aunt Kathy!

We miss you. We will let you know if we need anything. Ya'll are so precious to us. Thank you for lifting us up.

We are doing well. We start language study on Monday so you can remember that. We look forward to learning to communicate.

We love you, Wendy and Kevin

October 21, 2006

There is a Name for That

It amazes me how many people eat out these days. In Warner Robins, where we live, there is at least an hour wait for a table on any weekend night at any chain restaurant you happen to choose. I'm convinced not many people cook at home anymore. When I was growing up there was no such thing as chain restaurants. People ate at home, and I think we were better for it. The first steakhouse I ever saw was a Sizzlin' in Griffin, Ga. that we stopped at sometimes on the way to Braves games. We were all amazed that they cooked that many steaks for so many people.

The only place we had to eat out in Reynolds when I was a young boy was Crook's Restaurant which was owned by M.L. and Daisy Crook. We ate there many times on Sunday after church. In fact, most everybody in town ate there on Sunday after church.

One of my fond memories was that of a waitress that worked there named Bonnie Palmer. The memory is fond because she was the only person I ever saw who could write with either hand. Her handwriting was just as good with her left hand as it was with her right. She told me she learned to write with both hands because she was so busy taking orders at Crook's Restaurant that her right hand would give out, and she would use her left hand. I don't know if she was pulling my leg or not but that's what she always told me. There is a name for that by the way. It's called ambidextrous.

I later learned something else about this special lady. She never missed a day of school the entire time she was in school. Grades 1 thru 12 and never missed a day. There is a name for that too. It is called discipline.

Bonnie would later marry James Bailey. They had three children. They walked through a parent's worst nightmare. One of their small children died accidentally. There is a name for that too. It's called unbearable pain.

Several years ago James checked into a hospital to have what everyone thought was routine heart bypass surgery. He was not sick when he was admitted for that surgery, but he did have some blockages, and the doctor thought it best to do the bypass surgery. James went through the surgery and made it home. But he died a day or two have being dismissed from the hospital. There is a name for that as well. It's called intense grief.

Bonnie spent most of her adult life working at Blue Bird Bus Manufacturing Company. A few years after James passed away, Blue Bird went through some financial challenges which resulted in major job cuts. You guessed it. Bonnie lost her job, and there is a name for that. It's called "you've got to be kidding."

In spite of it all, Bonnie continued to have a smile on her face and kept her faith in a God she continued to trust in spite of her circumstances. There are two names for that. They are perseverance and faithfulness.

This weekend I stopped by the funeral home in Reynolds and saw Bonnie, who works there part-time.

In a little over a year, Bonnie has lost an amazing 85 pounds. If anybody has what it takes to lose that much weight, it would be Bonnie Bailey. There is a name for that. It's called incredible. And I am positive I saw a twinkle in her eye.

Bonnie is planning a trip to South Korea to visit her son Greg and his family, and she is beside herself because she will get to spend some time with her grandbabies. There is a name for that too. It's called excitement.

I don't know of anybody who deserves a little excitement more than Bonnie Bailey. Booker T. Washington said, "Success is to be measured not so much by the position one has reached in life as by the obstacles that one has to overcome while trying to succeed."

I really think Booker T. was exactly right. And if that is true, there is a word that perfectly describes this special lady. That word would be successful.

And there is a name for that. It's called greatness.

February 25, 2008

We Will Still Call Her Claire

Claire Underwood has just finished competing in what may be the toughest competition there is. This competition is not about who wins a race or a game of basketball or baseball or football. But it is a competition about potential leadership, and it is a competition of the mind and intellect in the realm of academia.

Claire is the daughter of Rudy and Carol Underwood of Marietta. Rudy is my wife's brother. Rudy and Carol are very proud of their youngest daughter this morning. And that pride has run about 100 miles down I-75 to Warner Robins, Ga. Claire's aunt and uncle in Warner Robins are just as proud.

This very well rounded gal with the keen sense of humor will graduate from high school in a few short months. In anticipation of that event, several universities have been competing with each other to get her to attend their institution in the fall.

The University of Georgia won that competition this past week. They landed a jewel. Claire has signed on the dotted line and will officially become a Georgia Bulldog, and trust me; she gets a free ride and more. Rudy and Carol can keep the money they have saved to send this girl to college.

Don't hold me to these facts but I don't think I will be far off. Around 16,000 high school seniors would have applied to become students at UGA when Fall Semester begins in 2007. About 5,000 will be accepted. The average grade point average will be around 3.8 and the average SAT score will be around 1240.

For the record, I graduated from UGA in 1976, but I would have never been accepted with those qualifications. I think my degree there is worth much more today than it was 31 years ago.

But to continue my story, of the 5000 students accepted at UGA, about 800 of the brightest are qualified to apply to be a Ramsey Scholar. Of the 800 who applied for that scholarship, only about 65 were chosen. As you can imagine the 65 who qualify as a Ramsey Scholar are very special folks. According to the UGA website, Ramsey Scholars have an average SAT score of 1522 and average high school grade point average is 4.27 on a 4.0 scale, which indicates extra points for Advanced Placement classes. Of the 65 who qualified as a Ramsey Scholar, only 20 were chosen as a Foundation Fellow. To say this select group is the cream of the crop is an understatement.

Claire Underwood was named a Foundation Fellow this week. It is the most prestigious scholarship offered at the University of Georgia. For the next four years, she will not only be studying at UGA, but she will be traveling all over the world.

I have no idea what she will be studying and where her life will take her. But one thing I'm fairly positive about today.

She will do very well.

And when she does we will still call her Claire.

But I have a strong feeling a lot of other folks will call her Boss.

March 04, 2007

There is a Recipe

You want to move up in your company? You want to be noticed? You want to be fulfilled when you lie in bed at night?

There is a recipe.

You begin with the foundation of integrity. You make it your business to show up at work earlier and work harder than everyone else. You never miss work unless you absolutely cannot be there. You keep challenging yourself to learn all you can about whatever you are doing. You never stop learning. You do what you say you are going to do. You can be counted on to deliver. You have fun in the process. You are always completely loyal to the people you work for.

I had several role models as a young man beginning a career after college. I was fortunate to have some people in my life who demonstrated some basic principles of success.

One of those was a lady who came to work with us about the time I graduated from college.

Blanche Perkins and her husband, Thomas, owned and operated Perkins Store about two miles south of Reynolds for many years. Thomas became ill and passed away, and the Perkins family eventually made the decision to close the store.

We immediately hired Blanche to work for us at our store. And it was the best decision we ever made.

Let me tell you why.

Blanche was a person of great integrity. She was as honest as the day is long. If she said she was going to do something, she did it. If she didn't think she could do it, she would tell you that too. She never pretended to be someone she was not. You never had to wonder how you stood with her.

Blanche had a work ethic like nobody I've ever known. She would show up earlier and stay later than the other employees. At the end of the day, as a cashier, she always took in about twice as much as the rest of the clerks. I have a strong feeling that she never went home after a day of work and had even a thought that she did not earn her pay that day. She earned it and she knew she earned it.

She also had great knowledge of the business. That did not come to her by osmosis either. During down times you would see her out in the store making sure she knew the prices. Although the price of each item was supposed to be on the item, she would know the price if it wasn't. She would also be the first to notice if someone had put the wrong price on an item. She had more knowledge than everyone else because she made a conscious decision to learn everything.

Blanche also had a sense of humor. She made it fun. She never did that at the expense of not going above and beyond our expectations at work, but she would play a joke on someone in a heartbeat. She was fun to be around, and she made it seem to others as if she was glad to be there. That attitude was contagious to others who worked there.

Webster's Dictionary should have Blanche's picture next to the word dependable. I never remember her being late for work, and I really don't remember her missing a day of work. If she did miss a day, you can bet your last dollar is was because there were circumstances beyond her control. You could just count on her.

Blanche was also very loyal to the people who wrote her paycheck. I'm sure there were times she was ready to wring my neck and my brother's neck, but nobody else would know it. She would fall on the sword for us. And we knew it.

Why do I tell you all this about Blanche Perkins?

Because it really doesn't matter if you work in a grocery store in Reynolds or if you are paid to teach kids to read at school or if you work for a large corporation in Texas or if you work in your home--the principles here apply.

Integrity, strong work ethic, desire for knowledge, sense of humor, dependability, and loyalty.

Blanche Perkins demonstrated all of that as well as anyone I have ever known.

And I sure am glad I got to rub shoulders with her for several years and learned her receipe.

September 20, 2006

I'm Giving It To You Straight

Ray's Paint and Body has a catchy phrase on their ads - *We Give It To You Straight.* In other words you bring in a crashed vehicle, they will give it back to you just as it was before you crashed it, and they will. I will give it to you straight right here. I promise not to beat around the bush. If some of you young readers pay attention to the next few paragraphs--what you read might just motivate you to forget the excuses and take responsibility for your own actions.

Ray Tiencken and I go back a long way. In fact, all the way back to elementary school. I have no doubt if I needed Ray at any hour of the night for whatever reason no matter where I happened to be, he would come to my rescue. He can buy whatever he wants, and he can write a check for it. He owns a house in Florida and one in Georgia. And he has earned every dime. Trust me, nothing was ever given to him. He pulled himself up by his own boot straps. His story is a story that should be told, and a lesson that should be learned.

Ray's dad Bill was one of the best body men you could possibly find. Bill had a body shop next to his house when Ray was growing up. He could definitely give it back to you straight even though he couldn't stay straight himself. Bill was an alcoholic. But even with that problem, he taught Ray everything he knows about body work. Maybe Ray had to finish the jobs because his dad couldn't, but for whatever reason, Ray learned how to do body work at a very young age.

Ray was driving by the age of thirteen. It was nothing to see him drive to school when we were in the 7th grade. He was the school bully and nobody messed with Ray Tiencken. In those days, Ray would rather fight that eat. And he got into more than a few fights along the way. As I look back on it, Ray was an angry kid and probably was taking his plight in life out on other kids. And he was tough as they come. Even after he became an adult he still loved to fight. He entered the first tough man competition at the Macon Coliseum years ago. There were no rules and no weight divisions. Ray weighed 180 pounds when he entered and had to fight a guy who weighed 230. Although Ray says he got the snot beat out of him, he refused to go down and refused to give up. He lasted all three rounds.

In life, he refused to go down and refused to give up. After working for his dad as a young man, Ray ended up working as the body man at several different car dealerships. Just like his dad, Ray had the reputation of being the best body man around. About 20 years ago Ray went in business for himself. It was the best thing he ever did. He worked hard and quickly used his talent to build a good business. He made money and invested his money back in his business. When he finally moved the business back to his hometown of Reynolds some 17 years ago, he had a booming business.

Early on Ray married his high school sweetheart, Martha Ellen, and they had two children. It was obvious Ray was determined to make it much easier for his kids than he had it growing up. And he did.

Just like his dad did years ago, Ray trained his son Toby in the same way he was trained. If you pull up to Ray's Paint and Body Shop (like I did yesterday), you will quickly notice this immaculate facility is not your normal paint and body shop. It is obvious that Ray has put a lot of money into the facility. He takes pride in the way his business looks. You will also quickly discover to the delight of his dad, Toby runs things now. Ray is still around to give advice and help out when he and Martha Ellen are not at their vacation home in Florida, but Toby is the man now. But I have a feeling Ray and Martha Ellen won't be too far away for a while because Toby and his new bride made them grandparents a few weeks ago.

As I talked to Ray yesterday, it dawned on me that he is not a man who is mad with the world anymore. He is not looking for a fight or even an argument. He is at peace with himself and at peace with the world, and he is at peace at where he is in life.

Ray never went to college. He was already working when the rest of us left for college. But trust me he did get an education. He worked his rear end off and learned a skill that eventually made him a lot of money. I would venture to say he has made more than most folks with advanced college degrees. The lesson here is that anyone can overcome obstacles to find success if they are determined to find it.

In the end, there are no excuses. We are responsible for ourselves.

Like the rest of us, Ray came to a crossroads in life as a young man. He had the choice to take the wide road and join the throngs of people with all the good excuses walking aimlessly through life just trying to get by. Or he could choose the narrow path of doing whatever it takes to make something of himself. Ray chose the narrow path. Always the road less traveled was the right path.

I am fortunate to have had the opportunity to have known a lot of successful business people in my life. But there are none I respect more than Ray Tiencken.

And I'm giving it to you straight.

May 26, 2007

Not an Underachiever

If you are a sports fan, you will undoubtedly pick up a newspaper tomorrow and read that Greg Norman choked again.

I'm sure you will read about the 1996 Masters when Norman, better known as The "Great White Shark," was leading by six strokes after three rounds only to lose by five strokes after a collapse on the final day that was voted by ESPN as the third biggest sports choke in the past 25 years. You will also probably read about 1986 when Norman led all four majors but won only one of them that year. Although he was ranked the number one golfer in the world for seven years, you will read that he is known as an underachiever.

Greg Norman won 87 professional golf tournaments in his career including the Players Championship and two British Opens. I don't think there are a whole lot of folks in the history of golf on that list. He has played in 88 major championships and won two, has had 8 second place finishes, 14 top three finishes, 20 top five finishes and 30 top ten finishes. In 1991, he was inducted into the World Golf Hall of Fame. Doesn't sound too shabby to me.

His business successes with companies like MacGregor Golf and Greg Norman Golf Design ain't too shabby either. He is worth hundreds of millions of dollars (or at least he was until his recent divorce). She probably got a hundred or two of that but I would think with his recent marriage to tennis legend Chrissie Evert, he got it back and more.

Norman's hobbies don't represent underachievement either. An avid offshore fisherman, Norman has owned several rather nice boats. His latest one has been better described as a ship. This underachiever that you will read about sold it for a reported $77 million dollars.

This week, only three weeks after his highly publicized marriage to Evert, he entered the British Open to practice for some senior events coming up. Although the Shark has played very little competitive golf in the last 10 years or so, I think his new found happiness in his marriage spurred him on to compete again.

When this 53 year old golf fan turned on the TV Saturday morning and saw that a 53 year old golfing legend was leading The Open, it got my attention. At the end of the day, this 53 year old so called underachiever was leading the entire field.

So the questions began. Would he falter again? Would the famous underachiever blow it again? The thought of him even putting himself in the position to lose again almost made me sick at my stomach. But winners always do that. I don't think I have ever pulled for a golfer as much as I was pulling for Norman today. When my preacher at church this morning asked us to bow our heads to pray, I said a prayer for the Shark. Not kidding. "God, let him win it for the all the naysayers."

He didn't win today.

But he is still a winner.

When he walked off the course today, I wasn't thinking underachiever. I was thinking class. When interviewed, he showed the graciousness of a true champion during the interview that he showed on the course all day. I literally had tears in my eyes.

But you will undoubtedly read somewhere that Norman again demonstrated he is an underachiever.

You show me any 53 year-old-man that has EVER led one of the four major golf tournaments after three rounds and I will, as my dad used to say, "run buck naked around the Henry Grady hotel."

I won't be doing that (thank goodness) because you will have a hard time finding that golfer.

In fact, that is a really short list. Greg Norman may just be the only man in the history of golf on that list.

Doesn't sound like an underachiever to me.

July 20, 2008

Note: I guess I better start getting ready to find the Henry Grady Hotel, because a year after Norman's feat, 59-year-old Tom Watson led the British Open until the final hole. He lost after a four-hole playoff. I wouldn't exactly call Mr. Watson an underachiever either.

Those Girls Could Play

I personally think it all started on the playground at Reynolds Elementary School. Maybe it started as we watched our heroes play basketball for the Reynolds High School Tigers. We wanted to be able to play just like them.

One thing is for sure. For a group of us, a pickup basketball game on the playground at Reynolds Elementary School was what we did almost every day.

I can still hear the chosen student of the day standing at the door of the north wing of the school yelling at the top of his or her lungs:

"Third grade coming in!"

Words like that were the final buzzer for many a basketball game at Reynolds Elementary. The game was over, and it was time to go back to the dreaded classroom.

Billy Bell and I would usually be the captains for the playground games, and we would choose the teams. We would flip a coin to see who would choose first. The winner of that coin flip already knew who would be chosen first to be on their team. The loser of the coin flip also knew who would be their first choice.

It was always the same. Bunny Fuller was chosen first and Sandra Arnold was next.

Then we started choosing the boys.

Make no mistake about it. Those two girls could play basketball, and we watched them get better and better as time went on. I like to think that playing with a bunch of boys on the playgrounds in Reynolds in their early years didn't hurt their abilities in the later years. I am certain they made us guys much better than we would have been if they had not played with us.

Although I attended a different high school, I always kept up with them as they went on to become superstars on the basketball court.

I looked for Bunny and Sandra in the box scores in the sports pages after every game. I also read about them often because they were written about often. I felt like they were my family, and for some reason, I thought our playground group at Reynolds Elementary somehow contributed to their success.

How good were they?

Let's just say the teams they played on from the 8th grade until their senior year in high school never lost a basketball game. The Lady Vikings of Taylor County High School in Butler, Ga. won 132 straight basketball games and five straight state championships. Bunny and Sandra starred on four of those.

That state record of 132 consecutive wins still stands today. Check it out for yourself.

For the record, Bunny and Sandra led teams that actually won more than 132 straight games because of their undefeated 8th grade season. I think their total is 146.

It didn't hurt that the legendary Norman Carter was their high school coach. He was a master motivator and teacher of the game. No matter how good the talent, you have to have someone great at the helm to have that kind of success, and you have to be able to take the good players and mesh them with the great players. Norman Carter did that as well as anyone. Anywhere.

As with any championship team, there were many who contributed. In fact, the girl who would later become my wife played on a couple of those championship teams and was actually on the starting line-up during that last championship year. Being on the starting line-up on that team was no small accomplishment.

Bunny went on to have a great basketball career at Middle Georgia College and the University of Georgia. Bunny was named Scholar Athlete at the University of Georgia in 1976. You will find her name inscribed at the top of a list on a monument behind the Coliseum in Athens among such names as Hershel Walker and Ray Goff.

There should be a monument somewhere in Taylor County about the greatest athletic accomplishments in the history of the county.

I have no doubt that the names of Bunny Fuller Harris and Sandra Arnold would be inscribed at the top of that list.

But if that monument is never erected, their names will always be indelibly inscribed in the minds of those who saw them play.

September 4, 2006

Two More Examples

I had the privilege of visiting with Dr. Hugh Sealy, MD, and his wife Connie for a few minutes on Friday. Dr. Sealy, a 1948 graduate of Duke University Medical School, is a retired well-known Cardiologist from Macon, GA.

Dr. Sealy has been a major force in the medical community in Middle Georgia for a lot of years now. He has served as President of the Macon Medical Society, served as Chairman of the Macon-Bibb County Hospital Authority and was Director of the Coronary Unit at the Medical Center of Central Georgia for many years. He and another local cardiologist joined together years ago to found the Georgia Heart Center. Dr. Sealy also served as a clinical professor of medicine at Mercer University.

Not bad for a country boy who grew up in Reynolds.

Interestingly Dr. Sealy had an older brother who also was a medical doctor. Dr. Will Camp Sealy graduated from Emory University Medical School in 1936. This Dr. Sealy served his internship at Duke University and completed the surgical residency program and eventually became a thoracic surgeon ... a famous one at that.

Dr. Will Camp Sealy, a true international pioneer in thoracic surgery, was featured in *Life* magazine in 1958 performing hypothermic cardiopulmonary bypass surgery. He also happens to be credited with developing the field of electrophysiology and is known worldwide as the "father of arrhythmia surgery." In 1968, this Dr. Sealy performed the first pathway ablation for Wolff-Parkinson-White Syndrome on the "fisherman with a fast pulse," which has been documented in detail internationally in medical journals.

Again, not bad for a country boy who grew up in Reynolds.

Dr. Will Camp Sealy graduated from Reynolds High School in 1929. Dr. Hugh, who I visited with yesterday, graduated from Reynolds High School in 1942.

A few weeks ago, I spoke at the 50th Anniversary Banquet of the Reynolds Kiwanis Club, now known as the Kiwanis Club of Taylor County. I spoke of the incredible success in their lives of the charter members and their families. The Sealy brothers had already left Reynolds before the Kiwanis Club was chartered, so they were not included in my remarks, but they are no doubt the most famous brothers who ever came out of Reynolds.

I was born and raised in Reynolds and the older I get the more I realize how fortunate I was to grow up there. I have written about this little town and spoken about it to thousands across this country.

The Sealy brothers' stories are two more examples of why I plan to continue doing that.

August 23, 2008

Remembering a Hero

When you are a little boy in the fourth grade, you are always looking for a hero. When I was growing up most heroes for boys that age were found in the form of an athlete.

I certainly had a hero. And he was quite an athlete.

He wore Number 42 on the basketball court. He was a catcher on the high school baseball team, and he was a runner and a pole-vaulter on the track team.

He just wasn't a little good at these sports. He was really good. He set the standard for the rest of the athletes on the team.

His name was Mike Brunson. He graduated from Reynolds High School in 1964.

And believe me, I watched his every move.

I have been trying to remember what made him so special in my eyes. When I look back, I know that there had to be other qualities besides being so good at sports that caused me to look up to him as a little boy.

I do remember that Mike was very humble. He would dominate in all sports but his athletic success never went to his head. He was always just Mike off the field. He was very laid back and it took a lot to get him excited. He just seemed to take everything in stride.

He also had a contagious smile.

The thing I remember the most is he took up time with me as a little boy. I absolutely loved visiting the Brunson's house with my mama. Mike would take me upstairs to his room and make me feel like I was the most important person in the world. He was 8 years older than me, but he treated me like I was his equal.

I never forgot that.

Mike left Reynolds and went on to become a pharmacist. He married his high school sweetheart, Sandy Hinton, and they owned a drug store in Columbus for many years. They raised two beautiful daughters.

Mike and Sandy became people of great faith. They made a huge impact in their world through their church.

Now he became a greater hero in my eyes.

Mike and Sandy eventually sold their drug store in Columbus and moved to Kansas.

Exactly six years ago today, Mike was working in a drug store in Kansas and started to feel like something was wrong. In his normal unassuming manner, he did not want to alarm anyone, so he decided to drive himself to the hospital. He suffered a heart attack on the way and did not make it.

He was 54 years old.

For the past six years, I have remembered Mike Brunson on September 7, and I say a prayer for the family he left behind.

When I remember him, I am reminded that I should never be too busy to take time for a child, and I am also reminded that humbleness is a sign of greatness.

That's the kind of stuff of which heroes are made.

September 7, 2006

The Greatest Among You

When I was a kid visiting my grandmother in Fort Myers, Florida we always visited her friend, Marion Smith. I mentioned the Whatleys from Reynolds during one of those visits, and she told me she had never heard of them. I could not believe what she said, and I remember my response.

"You mean to tell me you don't know the Whatleys??"

Marion later always laughed about that conversation and the fact that I thought at the time everybody in the United States knew the Whatleys.

I guess everybody doesn't know them. But I can tell you there are tens of thousands of people in 18 states that have heard of them now. I personally told them. I have mentioned them in every speech I have ever given.

Ed Whatley was one of two doctors in the town of Reynolds. He and Rosemary and their four children lived right next door to us all of my growing up years. I cannot imagine a life without the Whatleys next door.

Dr. Whatley was a servant. There is no other way to describe him. He could have practiced medicine wherever he wished and made much more money, but he chose to serve the people of Reynolds and Taylor County and the surrounding area.

He and Dr. Sams owned the local hospital. They saw patients all day long in their offices at the hospital and took care of the sick ones who were admitted there. They delivered babies (including this one) and were also general surgeons.

When they left the office every day, they went on house calls. They both worked all hours of the night, and they sacrificed every day for the sake of others. Seven days a week.

I remember many nights being sick when I was a child and Dr. Whatley would come by the house while making rounds to give me a shot. The people of our little town were spoiled rotten. You got sick - you would simply call Dr. Whatley or Dr. Sams and one of them would eventually get by to see you. It could be after midnight but he would get there.

Doctors just don't do that anymore ... anywhere. Can you imagine getting sick in the middle of the night and giving your doctor a call and asking him to come by your house to check on you and treat you?

Dr. Whatley retired several years ago. If anybody on earth deserved retirement, it was Dr. Whatley.

He and his wife still live in the same house next door to where I grew up.

When I go to Reynolds or through Reynolds, I always stop by to visit. I've had some great visits and a lot of laughs in the last few years since his retirement visiting at their house.

But it's not as fun as it used to be.

His beloved Rosemary is not doing too well these days. She has been in declining health for many months now. She is not getting better and it is not easy to watch.

But what is inspiring to watch is the way her husband looks after her.

He is quietly preaching one of the most powerful sermons I have ever heard or witnessed. And believe me, he is not preaching with flowery words or catchy phrases.

His sermon is one of love, patience and deed.

And if I have to make a list of the greatest people I have ever known, you would find Ed Whatley right at the top of that list.

The greatest among you will be your servant.

That's in the Bible, *Matthew* 23: 11 by the way.

August 25, 2006

Only One Still Standing

I started the first grade in the fall of 1960. I attended the first day and came home and told Mama I have been, and I am not going back. I didn't like the idea of having to stand in line to eat lunch and having to raise your hand to go to the bathroom. I sure didn't like drinking milk with my meal. I just wasn't used to that kind of stuff. I thought I was in prison.

Forty six years later and looking back, I'm glad Mama made me go back the next day.

The group of about 30 people I started to school with on that fall day in 1960 are special people to me. I attended a wedding this past weekend and ran into Bunny Fuller Harris and Will Crawley, who were both part of my original first grade class. I'm always reminded when I see any of our group that we really are like family. We have common roots and we share a whole lot of wonderful memories.

We also shared some of the best teachers who ever entered the profession.

They taught us reading, writing and arithmetic. I realized later on in high school and in college just how well they did that. I had an educational foundation that could be compared to anybody--anywhere.

But they taught us much more than that. The first items on the agenda each day were the Pledge of Allegiance, a reading from the Bible and a prayer. We also prayed and thanked God for the food before we were herded to lunch each day.

Some of our teachers were also our Sunday School teachers, and they were also our parents, grandparents or friends of our parents. In other words, if we got in trouble at school, you can be sure we would get in trouble again when we got home. We certainly could not hide a bad grade.

They taught us but they also cared about us.

When I came back years later and took over the funeral business in Reynolds, I had an interesting responsibility. One by one, I buried the group of people who had such a major impact on my life. I can tell you each time I had one of those funerals, I remembered what they had done for this little boy growing up in our special little town. And I had a grateful heart.

Most of them are buried within a rock's throw from each other in the city cemetery in Reynolds.

There is only one of those teachers still standing. Mrs. Ruth Jones, our sixth grade teacher is alive and well. In fact, I have her email address on my computer, and we email back and forth pretty much every week.

A few years ago we had a reunion of our original first grade class that went through 8 grades together at Reynolds Elementary. Miss Ruth came and even brought a few of her old grade books. We started the reunion with the Pledge of Allegiance and a prayer. She then did a roll call from the original class roll.

To say that group of people appreciated her presence would be an understatement.

Recently, Miss Ruth sent me an email and told me she had moved to Jamestown Assisted Living Facility in nearby Fort Valley.

A few emails later she asked if I ever worked for free. She then asked if I would consider coming to Fort Valley to speak to the residents of Jamestown at their weekly devotional meeting.

Consider it? I would pay her for the honor to go there.

I am a busy guy these days, but I can tell you I will never be too busy to do a favor for Miss Ruth Jones.

I owe her more than she knows.

July 30, 2006

Long Life, Riches and Honor

Since my wife is on a shopping trip this weekend with a bunch of ladies and having a large time I'm sure, I drove over to Reynolds this morning. I had a large time myself visiting with a very familiar little bitty lady.

The good Lord willing, Jessie Mae King will turn 100 in about four months. She has been a major part of my life from the moment I was born into the world.

She began working for my mom and dad in 1942. My siblings and I spent an awful lot of time with Jessie Mae King as we grew up. And years later my children spent an awful lot of time with the same lady.

Our lives have taken us in many different directions.

But we have never forgotten this special lady.

She spoiled us in so many ways.

Daddy always said if something happened to Mama he would marry her.

Lord have mercy she could cook. It just never got any better than sitting at a table with Jessie's fried chicken, rice and gravy, butter beans, fresh peas, hocake cornbread and sweet tea. Still today when I eat a piece of fried chicken, I compare it to Jessie's.

And none compares to it.

We never had to worry about who our babysitter would be if daddy and mama were going somewhere. It would always be Jessie. Those nights sitting at home with Jessie when our parents were gone were some of the fondest memories I have in life. We talked about everything under the sun.

I learned more than I could ever imagine.

I had to get older before I began to understand the wisdom of this lady. She never had much knowledge and she surely didn't have much education, but there is a huge difference between knowledge and wisdom.

I know a lot of smart, educated and seemingly successful people who are fools. I also know a lot of seemingly successful people who look down on people who are not as educated, and those who don't have much materially.

My lifelong relationship with Jessie Mae King taught me the insanity of such thinking.

Trust me, it doesn't matter how much money or things we have in this life. We cannot take one dime with us when we leave here. I have never seen a hearse pulling a U-Haul trailer, and most of the fine suits are split in the back when they lay you in the casket.

You hang around a funeral home most of your life, and you figure out the importance of material things.

I will also always remember Jessie's childlike faith. We try to figure things out and if we can qualify it and quantify it, we believe.

Jessie just believed.

I'll never forget when our son David was a little boy and was very sick. Kathy and I were young parents, and we were beginning to get nervous. We just couldn't get the high fever to break, and we were just about to take him to the emergency room.

I looked in the bedroom and saw Jessie kneeling beside his bed. She didn't use an extravagant prayer or flowery words. I stood at the door and watched and listened. Her prayer was simple:

"Jesus, Jesus, Jesus," she repeated about ten times very quietly.

In a few minutes, she walked out of the room, and I walked to the bed and put my hand on David's head and immediately felt the sweat.

The fever had broken.

She just believed and her childlike faith had a lot to do with all of us believing.

Today, as I sat and visited with Jessie I thought about her remarkable but simple life. I also thought about a verse in the third chapter of Proverbs.

Long life is in her right hand and in her left hand are riches and honor.

She has achieved all three.

And I believe God continues to let her live to help fools like me.

November 11, 2006

The Time Has Come

Several years ago I visited the Georgia Sports Hall of Fame in Macon. Being a huge sports fan, I was very impressed with what I saw there. But when I left, I was absolutely flabbergasted and scratching my head and was greatly disappointed. Because of my disappointment I never went back and truthfully never even had the urge to go back.

My flabbergasted state and my disappointment stemmed from the fact that there was not even a mention of the Taylor County Lady Vikings and their legendary coach Norman Carter. For the life of me, I cannot understand why Norman Carter has not been inducted in the Georgia Hall of Fame and why his amazing teams from 1967-72 are not even mentioned.

Last night the girls and their coach were honored in the community where it all happened. What happened, by the way, is they won 132 straight basketball games and five straight state championships over a period of 5 years. No basketball team in the state of Georgia has ever done that. Only three other teams in the United States have ever won that many consecutive games. The Taylor County Viking girls are not even mentioned in the Georgia Hall of Fame?

You've got to be kidding.

Norman Carter coached basketball in Taylor County for twelve years. About a year into his winning streak, he became Superintendent of the Taylor County School System. He asked permission from the School Board to let him continue coaching until he lost. That took a few years.

During the twelve years he coached in Taylor County, he won seven state championships. I haven't checked, but I wonder how many coaches in the history of our state have won a state championship in seven out of twelve starts. His teams won 340 basketball games, and lost only 31 during those 12 years. His record speaks for itself.

The selection committee should start with his record. That is enough. But while they are investigating, they should interview at least a few of the girls he coached. To the person, they will say that Norman Carter was one of the greatest influences in their lives. They will say that he taught them much more than basketball. But he taught them life lessons about hard work, how to work together, how to overcome obstacles, how to be prepared for the enemy, how to have priorities and most importantly, how to be a winner when most people don't want you to win. Or think you can't.

He even taught his players how to lose and how to come back when you've been knocked down. They didn't have much practice in the how to lose part. But when they finally did lose, that same team came back that same year and won another state championship, and that may be his greatest coaching accomplishment.

In a world where you read almost every day of sports icons having their character questioned because of wrong decisions leaving the kids who look up to them disillusioned, the selection committee in this case should go past just looking at the basketball record and the girls he coached and do a little more investigating.

I suggest they ride out to the Golden Rule in Taylor County and interview some of the girls there. Or better yet, interview a few of the girls who have already been through that program. This oasis for girls who have been "knocked down" because of chemical addiction was founded by Norman and Jane Carter in 1996. There are 45 girls there now and a waiting list much longer than that. Again Norman Carter is coaching and teaching girls the same lessons he taught 35 years ago on the basketball court. He is still teaching lessons about hard work, how to work together, how to overcome obstacles, how to be prepared for the enemy, how to have priorities and most importantly, how to be a winner when most people don't want you to win. Or think you can't.

Following is the Mission Statement for the Georgia Sports Hall of Fame:

Georgia Sports Hall of Fame serves to collect, preserve, and interpret the history of sports in Georgia. We honor those who, by their outstanding achievement or service, have made lasting contributions to the cause of sports in Georgia, the nation, and the world. Further, the Georgia Sports Hall of Fame seeks to maintain the high ideals and traditions of sports as a positive influence on the youth of our state, emphasizing sportsmanship, physical fitness, and leadership that sports teach.

If Norman Carter doesn't fit that bill, they need to think about changing their mission statement.

I think it is time for the people of Taylor County and others who know and appreciate Norman Carter and what he has accomplished through Georgia sports to be heard.

It is time for a full court press.

As I was looking around the room last night, his students are not getting younger. If the crowd who was gathered last night doesn't lead the charge, it will never happen. The next generation won't have the luxury of first-hand knowledge of his accomplishments.

We owe it to ourselves. We owe it to Coach Carter, and we owe it to the people of our great state. The story of Norman Carter and his amazing Lady Vikings of Taylor County must be preserved in the history of sports in Georgia.

The time has come.

March 18, 2007

Note: My wife's former coach, mentor and lifelong hero, Norman Carter, was inducted into the Georgia Sports Hall of Fame on February 26, 2008. We, along with a throng of folks from Taylor County, Ga., attended the banquet in Atlanta. I take back everything I said about their selection committee. I applaud them. In fact, they deserve a standing ovation. The story of Norman Carter and his unmatched accomplishment in high school sports in the state of Georgia will be forever told in the Georgia Sports Hall of Fame. It was long overdue but right on time.

Little League but Large Lessons

I don't remember how it all began but the five years I'm about to tell you about are no doubt some of the fondest memories I have as a boy growing up in Reynolds. I think it was the first formal little league organization in the history of Reynolds. Youth baseball had been played since the beginning of time in Reynolds but I don't think it had ever been quite like this. By the way, the Reynolds Little League was not a budgeted item in county or city government. It was started, organized and maintained by a few parents who cared about the kids in town. I was fortunate enough to be one of the beneficiaries of their care and concern.

The parents who cared and sacrificed who come to my mind are people like Willie Gaultney, Hubert Arnold, Bo Bo Bartlett, W.T. Williams and Pat Patterson. If I remember correctly, Mr. Willie was the chief organizer. I know there were others but these men were always there. They were sacrificing their Saturdays and many evenings after work to make sure the kids had this opportunity.

There were four teams: The Giants, the Indians, the Yankees and the Dodgers. The ages of the players ranged from age 8 to age 12. The uniforms were first class. There were no, "I need $15 for the shirt--you go buy the pants" speeches at the beginning of the year. The professional jerseys and baseball pants and the stirrup socks all matched, and they were all paid for by local merchants. The schedules were not printed on sheets of paper and handed out. Instead they were printed on professional cards paid for by local politicians with their ads on the back. Schedules in which the Atlanta Braves would be proud.

The league started in the summer of 1963. Major league baseball had real heroes in those days like Mantle, Mays, Aaron, Musial, Koufax and Drysdale. I was 8 years old going on 9 and already a huge baseball fan. But as a player, I had to play against boys who were 12 years old going on 13. I can still remember the horror of having to face the much older fireball pitcher named Steve Peacock. Local attorney and lifelong friend Chuck Byrd still has nightmares of the day he was hit by a Steve Peacock fastball. Years later when Steve worked for the City of Reynolds and I was the local undertaker, I was still intimidated by him. I also remember facing the southpaw Wayne McInvale. He didn't throw quite as hard, but it was plenty hard enough with no control. Wayne hit about 3 or 4 batters per game. I made sure my helmet was on securely when I faced Wayne. For any of you tourists who drive through Reynolds, Fort Wayne is the only motel in town. Fort Wayne's owner is former left handed wild man by the name of Wayne McInvale. You can eat there and you can stay there, but I would not advise standing in the batter's box against him.

The interesting thing about this Reynolds little league was the younger guys would get better and better as the years continued. For instance, by the time I was 10, facing guys two years older was a piece of cake. And by the time my group was 12, we would now dominate the league. We had paid our dues, learned by a lot of hard knocks and now were pretty doggone good baseball players.

As I look back there are a couple of lessons I learned from my incredible little league experience.

First, it doesn't hurt to be put in situations in life where we are overwhelmed. We learn how to survive, and the experience provides us with enormous opportunity later. We may not appreciate the short term benefit of those circumstances but the cumulative effect is rather amazing. No different from when I first started working for corporate America 10 years ago. I was completely overwhelmed, but I survived and the cumulative effect of many uncomfortable experiences made it possible for me to do what I am doing today. If I was never put in a situation where I was stretched beyond my ability, I don't think I would ever have even a chance to grow to my potential. I still appreciate the "overwhelming moments" this life always has a way of providing.

Secondly, the importance of organized youth sports can never be underestimated. Not only do young kids learn about teamwork, personal success and how to keep going when there has been a temporary failure, but the memories of the people who played with them will stay with them the rest of their lives. Contrary to some opinions, the purpose is not to make major league players. The odds of that happening are about the same as winning the lottery. The purpose is to teach lessons to kids about teamwork and accountability and to learn about the thrill of victory and the agony of defeat. One thing is for sure: There will be plenty of both as their lives continue.

Amazingly it has been 44 years since the great men and leaders I have mentioned thought enough of the kids and our community to start our very organized and first class little league in Reynolds. Most of these guys have gone on to glory now.

But the investments they made are still paying off.

Little League but large lessons.

June 23, 2007

Champions of the World

(Warner Robins, Ga.) About 15 people went absolutely nuts in my den tonight when Dalton Carriker hit a shot over the right field fence in the bottom of the eighth inning to make our Warner Robins team the Little League World Series Champions. I know the same thing happened in dens throughout Warner Robins tonight, and I have a feeling the same thing happened in many dens throughout the United States.

I have been fortunate to experience many special moments in sports in my lifetime. I will put the accomplishment of this Warner Robins team up there with any of them. It was a team effort, and they won with class and great sportsmanship.

The scene after the game tonight fully illustrates the class I'm talking about. The Japanese team was devastated and most were weeping as most 12 year old boys would after giving such a monumental effort and coming up short. The Warner Robins boys were hugging them and consoling them and congratulating them. Our boys realized that either team could have won that game and both teams were great to even be playing in it.

I felt the same way after the Lubbock, Texas game. I realize that Lubbock fully expected to win that game, and I felt sorry for the kids that lost. They were 18-0 in post-season play going into the U.S. Finals, and they had tremendous talent up and down that lineup. They are truly champions.

However, the Lubbock manager did not appear to be a champion. I also think the kids on that team and their families deserve better.

I began to form my opinion when I heard a comment he made in the dugout after an inside pitch by a Warner Robins pitcher. I heard the word "payback." The television announcer immediately said, "Did he just say what I think he said?" The pitch was a hanging curve ball, and the batter turned the wrong way on the ball. There was no way it was intentional and the announcer said the same. Taking the high road the announcers never mentioned his comment again. Later in the game, the Lubbock manager came out to the mound when our pitcher was batting and was overheard telling the pitcher, "This guy is the one who came inside on you." It was obvious the kid didn't know what he was talking about. But the manager thought it was time for payback. I guess I need to remind you these are 11-12 year old kids he is talking to about payback– not major leaguers.

I was further amazed, when I read his comments after the game where he commented that his Texas team was better than Warner Robins (after losing 5-2). I couldn't believe it. He went on to say that he saw better pitching in the regionals, and when asked to predict who would win the game between Georgia and the Japanese his answer was and I quote, "Japan will win that ballgame."

Maybe his team is better than the Georgia team, but they were not better that day. And maybe he saw better pitching in his regional tournaments, but he didn't lose to those pitchers. He did lose to ours. All he had to say is that his team came up a little short; they played a very good Georgia team, and they wish them the best in the game against Japan and will be pulling for them. But he did not show a lot of class with his comments, and I hope the parents of the great kids of Lubbock Texas noticed.

So when Dalton Carriker hit the game winning home run tonight to beat a very great Japanese team after two extra innings of play, I jumped and yelled for two reasons. The first was because I was pulling for our team, and I couldn't believe they had won it all. They deserve all the yelling and screaming that was going on in our den and throughout our state tonight.

But the other reason I was jumping and yelling was because the boys of Warner Robins had proven the Lubbock manager wrong. In my view the Japanese boys are winners and the Lubbock boys are winners. But the Lubbock manager is not and he could learn a lesson or two from the kids.

And whether he likes it or not, the boys of summer from Warner Robins, Ga. are champions of the world. And this town will most definitely go crazy when they get home.

August 26, 2007

Sometimes Overwhelming Pays Off

(Houston, Texas) Overwhelming moments in life are good for us. Although very uncomfortable in the short run, those moments have a cumulative effect that can end up to be very positive forces in our lives.

Tonight, Lee Longino and I had dinner together. I was reminded of that life lesson. About eight years ago, which was a couple of years after I joined the ranks of Corporate America, Lee Longino became my Regional President. Being a small town funeral home operator who had only a few funeral home locations to oversee, the Regional President was not only a long way from me physically (from Georgia to Houston) but also a long way up the totem pole of the company for which I was employed. I had met Lee a few times at meetings in Houston, but I did not know him well. I knew him well enough to know that he was a very smart and creative young man, and I was very confident that there was no way I had the capacity to do his job. I remember attending meetings and wondering how in the world he kept up with all he had to keep up with.

One day about seven years ago, my boss at the time called me to tell me he was resigning from the company to pursue another opportunity. I was totally shocked and was nervous about who would replace him. My boss had taught me a whole lot about the workings of Corporate America, and I had a great relationship with him. My fear was his replacement might not be quite as patient with me. I nervously wondered what would happen.

To my surprise, a week or so later I got a call from Lee Longino. He wanted me to fly to Houston to be interviewed for the possibility of taking my boss's place. I couldn't believe I would be considered for such a job in the first place. This job was a big one and included operational responsibility for several states, and I wondered if it was over my head. On the way to Houston that week, it dawned on me that I had never been to a job interview in my life. I had always worked for myself. When I sold the funeral homes, I came on with the company as an Area Manager but had never been interviewed. I began to get a little nervous about what he could possibly ask me.

When I arrived at his office that morning I was wearing my best suit and attempting to exhibit my best behavior. When I entered Lee's office I could not help but notice the glass walls and the gorgeous view of downtown Houston. Lee had a lady who I knew (and is now one of my favorite people) in the office to take notes. I was thinking that this sure is a long way from Goddard Funeral Home and Goddard Factory Direct Furniture in Reynolds. I sat down next to Carol the note taker. Lee was sitting behind his very large glass desk. We said our "hellos and how you doings" and then Lee told me he was going to ask me a few questions. I'll never forget the first question he asked me: "Bruce, if you take over the job as Area Vice President of the Southeast Region, what changes would you make and why?"

The first answer that came to my mind came right out of my mouth: "World peace… Definitely world peace." As Lee spewed coffee out of his mouth and Carol started laughing out loud, I tried to explain. I told them I thought for a moment I was a finalist in a beauty pageant.

We went on to have a fairly lengthy conversation about the funeral and cemetery business. And I was hired for this job. When I took on this new responsibility, I had never been so overwhelmed in my life. I decided I was going to work harder than everybody else and do my absolute best to try to figure out what I had to do. I can tell you those next few months were no different than when I was 8 years old trying to bat against 12 year old Steve Peacock's fastball. I was overwhelmed but it was very good for me. I learned a heck of a lot over a period of time.

Today my job responsibility is much greater than it was when I got that big promotion. Lee Longino and I have the same job title now, and we are peers. There was a time when I could not even comprehend the possibility of doing what he did. But I now realize I had the capacity to do more than I thought I could do. I have since thanked Lee for giving me a shot at doing what he thought I could do, but I could not even imagine. There have been others who have helped me along the way, but Lee gave me my first shot. He saw something in me that I could not see myself. He put me in an overwhelming situation. It was a situation where I could have easily made a fool of myself.

But as I've said so many times before: One can never have a chance at winning until he gets to the place where he is not afraid to lose.

Sometimes overwhelming pays off.

June 25, 2007

You Go Girl!

This is another one of those stories where I did not get permission from the person I am writing about. I would guess this person would be very nervous tonight if she knew I was writing about her, but I am writing about her anyway.

Since I spent about 4 years of my life and about 10 years of my dad's money in Athens, I have a little bit of knowledge about college life and specifically fraternities and sororities. They are social organizations where guys and girls from different parts of the state and country live together and socialize together and build enduring relationships with each other as they work toward getting a college degree.

I did some stupid things when I was in college and an active member of Lambda Chi Alpha fraternity. Knowing what I know now, I would definitely do a few things differently. But if I had to do it all over again, I would join the same fraternity. The friendships created and the lessons learned during those years far outweigh the stupid stuff I did.

I have noticed that a large majority of my fraternity brothers turned out to be very successful in life. I didn't realize it at the time, but I was hanging around some fairly outstanding folks. Some were crazy during those years but outstanding nonetheless.

One of my greatest accomplishments was making the starting lineup as a freshman on the fraternity intramural basketball team. When you think about competing with 125 outstanding guys – most of whom were great athletes… and make that team--it was no small accomplishment.

But that accomplishment does not compare to the accomplishment of the few guys who were elected officers of that fraternity. (I never was elected an officer by the way). The officers are chosen by their peers to ultimately be in charge of the rest of the group, and it is quite an honor to be chosen.

Running a college fraternity or sorority is much different that being an officer at a high school club where your only duty is to call a meeting to order and have some degree of knowledge about *Robert's Rules of Order*. College fraternities and sororities are big business. The President has personal responsibility for what goes on and has legal liability when what goes on is not what is supposed to go on. Further, there is fiscal responsibility for a budget that can be as much as a medium size business. College fraternities and sororities have been the training ground for a number of folks who went on to run big companies and do big things in life. If you interviewed a dozen or so folks who served as President of their college fraternity or sorority, I think you will find being elected to that position was one of their great honors in life. In most cases, that experience was the springboard that launched them into much bigger responsibilities and opportunities.

Which brings me to the subject at hand.

I found out today that my niece, Courtney Underwood, was elected yesterday as President of the Zeta Tau Alpha sorority at the University of Georgia. I can tell you that is a HUGE honor.

I think her dad is a little nervous about the responsibility that comes with the position, but Courtney is no doubt up to the challenge. She will be ultimately responsible for a budget in the hundreds of thousands of dollars and over 200 members. And she will be legally responsible for all the activities of the sorority.

But all that is okay. There is a price you pay for being a leader. Courtney will be the best President ZTA has ever known, and she will graduate and move on to even bigger and better things. She is a born leader and has the looks, personality and smarts to accomplish anything in life.

Congratulations to Courtney! You go girl!

You have made your entire family very proud. And I have a strong feeling this is only the beginning.

November 05, 2007

Why Most People Are Not Heart Surgeons

While Oprah gave away some of her favorite things at the Macon City Auditorium on Saturday, my wife and I had dinner on Saturday night with some of our favorite people.

Brad and Tessa Hobbs have been part of our church home group for several years and have become like family to us. As part of our family, we just have a blast when we hang out with them. And we are honored that a young couple like this couple would want to hang out with old folks like us.

Tess is a kindergarten teacher in the Houston County School system. Brad is a third year medical student at Mercer University School of Medicine. I think you can sense the talent.

They are living mainly on Tess' income these days because it would be rather difficult for a full-time medical student to hold down a paying job. So they have to count their pennies, live within a very strict budget and hold off on having babies while many of their friends have much more disposable income and have little ones in the oven or in the world. Thus the discipline.

Brad is leaning toward being a cardiothoracic surgeon, which is in simpler terms – a heart surgeon. That means after finishing medical school in 1 ½ years, he will have to complete a general surgery residency that will last at least 5 years and then a cardiothoracic fellowship that will last another 2 to 3 years, according to how many chests he cracks during that fellowship. You can do the math, but it will take at least 8 ½ years before Brad reaches his goal, and he really won't get paid very much in the meantime. I think you are getting a picture of their patience.

Yep, as usual there is a lesson here for the rest of us somewhat talented, undisciplined and impatient folks. If you really want to get somewhere in life, you have to be willing to pay the price, and in paying the price, it takes a little talent, a lot of discipline and large dose of patience.

Brad's biggest concern is being able to pay off the debt he is incurring for the expense of medical school. I looked up this morning what the average heart surgeon makes. My mathematical conclusion is that Brad can relax. He will be able to pay off the debt in rather short order.

Whatever they eventually earn, he and Tess will deserve it. They are both sacrificing now. The rewards will come later. This very talented couple understands that really well. But in the microwave mentality ("I want it now") world we live in, most people don't get that.

I suppose that is why most people are not heart surgeons.

November 18, 2007

Note: Brad decided not to be a heart surgeon and is currently serving his residency in Little Rock, Ark. specializing in Ear, Nose and Throat. They had a baby and have another on the way.

May This Sundial Always Mark the Time (and Reynolds)

I've tried my best to communicate that the little town of Reynolds is a remarkable place. Maybe some of you are beginning to believe me. As I have written before, Reynolds, population 1,200, is unique because of the people it has produced.

Case in point is Bill and Ann Howard Whatley. Bill is a retired Atlanta architect. The Whatleys still live in Atlanta, but they also have a house in Reynolds where they visit often. Somewhere around the city limits of Reynolds there must be a huge magnet that keeps attracting its natives back. Ann Howard Whatley, Bill's wife, is a native of Reynolds. She was a 1947 graduate of the University of Georgia. Her dad (another Reynolds native), J. Howard Neisler, was a 1908 graduate of UGA. He also happened to be the President of the Class of 1908. In case you don't have your calculator close by, that was exactly 100 years ago.

And exactly 100 years ago, Howard Neisler presented a sundial to the University on behalf of the Class of 1908. As President of the class, it was his job to oversee the erection of the sundial. He did and was proud that his class was responsible for it. A sundial, by the way, is a device that measures time by the position of the sun. You don't see many of those being made any more, and that is exactly what makes this story interesting.

In 1971, the sundial was stolen. It was probably some college prank or maybe it was someone who felt like they really needed a sundial. But for whatever reason the sundial that was placed by Howard Neisler where the famous Tombs Oak once stood has been missing for the past 36 years.

Over a year ago, the descendants of J. Howard Neisler, led by Bill and Ann Howard, decided they would purchase a new sundial in memory of their loved one. They quickly found out that would not be an easy task. As you might imagine, there are very few people who design and create brass sundials these days. Bill and Ann's son, John Whatley, who happens to be an American Airlines pilot, finally found a sundial designer by the name of Tony Moss in Bedlington, England. Moss used a black and white photograph of the original and created a face similar in size and appearance to the original but much richer in detail. The newly-created one incorporates modern scientific knowledge that makes it almost as accurate as a clock.

They were fortunate to find Tony Moss. When John flew to England to bring the new sundial back to the states, Mr. Moss said that would be the last one he would produce.

The sundial is back in its original spot in front of the Chapel on the University of Georgia campus. The sundial that was originally placed on that spot 100 years ago but has been missing for 36 years.

Interestingly, Howard Neisler died a couple of years before the sundial was stolen. But the memory of this remarkable man did not die. Nor did this family forget the sundial that was a symbol of an important part of his life.

In his original speech presenting the sundial, Mr. Neisler said, "This year the class of 1908 will leave as its testimonial a sundial. It selects this as a symbol that, as the dial's pointer traces the sun's course from its rise to its setting, so shall the memory of the University ever exert a beneficent influence on us throughout our whole lives. May this sundial never mark the time when our love for the University will have grown cold, or our services in her behalf have ceased to be a pleasant and a sacred duty."

So shall the memory of J. Howard Neisler ever exert a beneficent influence on his children and children's children and all who knew him and who will learn about him, and may the sundial placed in memory of him never mark the time when our love for those who have gone before us and blazed the path for us will have grown cold.

By the way, next time you are on the North UGA Campus, look closely at the new sundial. In the reconstruction process, the aviator grandson that commissioned the artist who designed the new sundial made sure everyone can find Reynolds. There is a little notch on the sundial that indicates the direct path to our great little town. Check it out.

July 30, 2008

May We Never Forget

My dad served in the Navy in World War II. As I got older I began to really appreciate the stories he told about the time he served as Lieutenant on the USS Mendocino. He loved his country and he had great respect for those who sacrificed life and limb for the cause of our freedom.

Last night I found a letter my dad wrote to his mother-in-law while in port at an island somewhere in the South Pacific. He talked about looking forward to coming home and joining his dad in the family business in Reynolds.

He was able to do that and lived a great life and raised a family in his hometown of Reynolds. He always said he was a better man for serving our country. But the truth is many of those brave Americans defending our country do not make it back.

One of those heroes who never made it back was a Second Lieutenant Army Air Force Fighter Pilot from Reynolds by the name of Benjamin Hodges. He was shot down defending a little village in France on June 20, 1944, exactly two weeks after D-Day.

Ben also had a brother in the Navy. Walton Hodges, Jr. flew torpedo planes off aircraft carriers. Walton Jr., who I knew well, made it back to Reynolds and raised his family there.

Benjamin's death not only broke a mom and dad's heart but he also left a young wife from Reynolds by the name of Dorothy Brunson Hodges. She would later marry another fighter pilot who served in World War II.

My dad always spoke with much pride and respect for the Hodges brothers and their service to our country in World War II. There is a marker for Benjamin Hodges at Hillcrest Cemetery in Reynolds on the Hodges lot. My dad told me years ago that Benjamin's boots are all that is buried there.

I found out today through an email that his foot is buried in St Laurent, Normandy, France at the American Cemetery, the cemetery depicted in the motion picture, *Saving Private Ryan.* His body is buried with his plane in a soggy area in a little village in France. The mayor of that town owns that property. Some cousins of the Hodges brothers visited the burial site in Normandy and the site of the crash in Rouy-le-Petit recently. They left some Georgia red clay at his grave in Normandy and also at the crash site. They explained to their tour guides that the crash site reminded them of Reynolds.

This town in France is planning on honoring Benjamin for sacrificing his life while defending their town from the Germans over 62 years ago. They are delighted to hook up with his relatives in the United States and get information they had no idea they would ever get. Some of the Hodges family are planning on going to France for that ceremony.

My dad would be absolutely flabbergasted that the world would ever become small enough to make this connection. The Internet truly is amazing.

In a day when many young people in our country are looking to movie stars, athletes and rock stars as heroes, I thought it would be good to introduce some real heroes.

Eugene Walton and Winifred Newsom Hodges produced two of them. From the little town of Reynolds, their two sons (Benjamin and Walton, Jr.), who were two years apart in age, became fighter pilots in two different branches of the service at the same time during the same war.

One of them is being honored in a little town in France for his heroic actions.

Both of them are being honored by the son of one of their best friends.

May we never forget.

December 27, 2006

Gena

You have seen her image in the aisles of your local supermarket. If you live in Atlanta or San Francisco or Minneapolis or Philadelphia or New York or Chicago or other places too numerous to mention, you might have seen her cooking on the morning television shows or even heard her on the radio.

Or maybe you received her bestselling book, *Gourmet Made Simple*, as a Christmas present. Or maybe you read about her and the company she and her husband founded in one of the many national magazines in which she has been featured.

Or maybe you are like me and watched her grow up in the not so populated town of Reynolds. Maybe you noticed her as a little girl selling peaches and produce out of the back of a pickup truck in the middle of town. Or maybe you noticed her babysitting little kids like my niece and nephew to make a few extra dollars. Or maybe you saw her as she got older and more and more beautiful running through the streets of Reynolds--always in shape and always pushing herself.

Or maybe you knew her at the University of Georgia where she received a degree in Landscape Architecture. Or maybe you knew her when she lived in Sea Island, Ga. as she began her career in her field of study.

Maybe you already know Gena.

But just in case you don't, Gena Neely Knox--daughter of Tommy and Joan Neely, has hit the big time. Her company, Fire and Flavor, is one of the fastest growing private companies in the United States. To be exact, *Inc.* magazine has Fire and Flavor ranked 264th of the 5000 fastest growing companies and Number 8 in the Top 100 Food and Beverage companies.

If you are not yet impressed with this Reynolds gal, you should also know Gena was chosen in 2008 by *Georgia Trend* magazine as a finalist in their 40 under 40 list, which represents the brightest and best among the rising young leaders in Georgia.

To make a great story short, Gena developed a love for cooking from her mom. In fact, she got her looks and her cooking talent from her mom. After she married, she continued to explore interesting food concepts as she cooked for her hubby or entertained friends. She read an article one day on a traditional Native American cooking process called "plank grilling." After some effort, she finally found some planks to purchase. Her husband and their friends loved the exceptional taste of food grilled on a plank, but Gena continued to have a difficult time finding retailers that sold the planks.

So Gena decided to make her own. Similar to her childhood experience of selling fruit and vegetables off the back of a pickup truck, she packaged her planks and took them to sell at the Atlanta Merchandise Mart. She wound up making $6,000 from sales in two days. What began as a small venture quickly grew into a large business. Davis and Gena Knox officially founded Fire and Flavor in September of 2003, and the rest is history.

In addition to planks, Fire and Flavor has now expanded its offering to an array of cooking products, including grilling papers and skewers, gourmet seasoning salt blends and rubs, and brining mixes.

As that company expands, the little town of Reynolds expands its claim for being the launching pad for some of the most amazing folks you would ever want to know.

Gena might be in a class all by herself.

January 12, 2009

Basket Four
Knowing People

"…you sure can learn a lot from other folks if you just take the time to know them or live by intention to find them. In my view, God puts people in our path for a reason. Sometimes those people can be 'upfront and on a stage', sometimes they can be acquaintances we just never take time to really know and sometimes they can be people you would never expect to be there to impact your life."

Sunshine

It rained in Reynolds all day today. The sunshine disappeared sometime Thursday afternoon when word spread that Tommy Mattingly had passed away.

I'm not sure who gave "Sunshine" Mattingly his name, but whoever did pegged him very well. Sunshine never met a stranger in his life, and he brightened up many a day for a lot of folks who crossed his path during his short 45 years on earth.

Although, Tommy could brighten up most anybody's day, the sun didn't always shine brightly in his own life. In fact, he probably experienced more dreary days than most folks I've known.

But he would never let you know it.

I first met the little boy who would become known throughout Taylor County as "Sunshine" when he was just a baby boy. The night before I met him, I had ridden over to the train station in Macon with my dad and Sunshine's Uncle Dennon to pick up Sunshine's mother who was coming in on a train.

We rode in the hearse.

His mother, Patricia, had walked through her garage a few mornings earlier wearing a night gown. There was an open gas can in the garage. When the night gown brushed against her car, the static electricity ignited the gas in the can and the gown she was wearing. She never had a chance.

This young mother left behind five small children. These little children ended up moving back to Reynolds to be raised by their grandparents, and there were some aunts and uncles who also greatly contributed to the raising.

I always felt close to the Mattingly kids. Although I was a young teenager myself when their mom died, I was never able to escape that mental image forty years ago of five little children sitting under that tent at the cemetery with their young mother's casket in front of them.

I watched Sunshine grow up, and I always made a point when I saw him to stop and talk and let him spread a little of his sunshine on me.

Sunshine has suffered through many physical problems the last few years. More than most 40-something-year-olds ever experience.

Not long ago I was about to walk into a store in Warner Robins and I heard someone yell "Bruce Goddard" as I walked toward the door. Sunshine was sitting in a car. I must have visited with him at least 15 minutes that day standing outside his car.

The last time I saw Sunshine was at Ft. Wayne Store in Reynolds where he worked behind the counter. His color didn't look good and I was thinking it must be difficult for him to be on his feet all day working. But, typical Sunshine, he never let me know he was not feeling well.

Despite his own troubles he was determined to keep spreading the sunshine.

When I heard about Sunshine's death, I couldn't help but think about that horrific scene at Mt. Olive Cemetery I have carried with me most of my life. But then I thought of a much better image of Sunshine being introduced at the Pearly Gates to a Mama he never had an opportunity to know.

The sunshine definitely disappeared in Taylor County yesterday afternoon.

But it was shining very brightly on the other side a millisecond later when this Mom got to embrace her boy.

March 27, 2009

Miracle Man

I don't think God makes folks like He used to make them. If He does, I certainly don't know where they are. When I look back over my life, I realize I was very fortunate to know and rub shoulders with some rather amazing people when I was a young man.

Mr. Cincinnatus Dugger Lucas, better known as "Mr. Nat," was definitely one of them.

Mr. Nat never had to worry about whether a financial institution was going to foreclose on his home. He never had a mortgage. In fact, he lived all his life in the house his father built when he married his mama. For those of you who like numbers, Mr. Nat lived in the same house for 99 years.

I think it would be safe to say that Mr. Nat did not like being indebted to anyone. I have a strong feeling he never was.

He was never concerned about airport delays or whether an airline was going to charge extra for checked luggage. In his 100 years and 6 months on this earth, he never traveled farther than the north Georgia Mountains and Florida.

Mr. Nat Lucas meant it as a young man at the wedding altar when he said "till death do us part." He was married to one woman for 67 years. His beloved wife Sara died in 1985. I remember the funeral well because my wife was very pregnant with our third and last child at the time of that funeral and I was wondering if I, the undertaker, would get the call from my wife before the funeral was done. She had our baby the day after the funeral and the Lucas family was the first to send a beautiful arrangement of flowers to her hospital room.

I never forgot that.

Mr. Nat spent almost his entire life farming land that had been in his family since the Civil War days. Like most of the farmers in the well-to-do Crowell Community outside of Reynolds, he was a very successful farmer. A man growing up in the late 1800's and early 1900's didn't have a lot of educational opportunities, but that never stopped him from learning. He consumed newspapers and kept up with news on television with great interest throughout his years. He had a great memory and neighbors and visitors were amazed at his excellent recall of people and their stories that happened years earlier.

If there was ever a steward of the land it was him. Among other things, he grew corn, cotton, peaches, pimento and pepper. He also raised cattle, hogs and chickens, and he made a lot of money along the way. He also served as Justice of the Peace for 40 years. As you might imagine, he was an avid fisherman and hunter.

Mr. and Mrs. Nat Lucas also raised children. And they did an incredible job doing that as well. They had two sons and two daughters and all ended up to be very successful folks very active in their churches and communities. Three of the four children celebrated their 50th wedding anniversary with their spouses (one of the daughters never married). They had seven grandchildren, eight great grandchildren, and at last count, 8 great-great grandchildren.

Mr. Nat had a physical constitution unheard of these days. When he was a young man he had a ruptured appendix. His father had to take him by train to a Macon hospital where he was confined many weeks. In the late 1940's he cut his arm through broken glass and severed arteries while attempting to push off his pickup truck. He drove himself the eight or so miles to the hospital. In the late 70's, he had a horrific head on collision with a big truck moving a mobile home and he almost bled to death.

Mr. Nat had a mind of his own and didn't mind giving orders and liked to do things his way. When he had the automobile accident, though barely alive, he first refused to let them put him in the ambulance at the accident scene because his funeral home of choice was not there to pick him up. In those days, ambulances and hearses were one in the same. When they finally got him to the local hospital, Dr. Whatley had to ride in the back of the ambulance with him to the Macon Hospital to keep him alive. Although confined to the hospital for several weeks after the accident, he somehow recuperated and came back strong.

Dr. Whatley called him the Miracle Man.

Mr. Cincinnatus Lucas died on June 7, 1992. His grandsons served as pallbearers. At the graveside, I noticed his casket was facing the wrong direction on the lowering device. I explained the problem to the grandsons after the service and asked them to hang around after the crowd dispersed so we could turn the casket around.

One of the grandsons laughingly said later that he could almost hear his Grandpa speaking from his casket, "Can't y'all do one last thing right?"

The truth is Mr. Nat Lucas did an awful lot right in his lifetime. All of us would do well to take a long look at the example he set. As I said, God just don't make folks like him anymore.

By the way, if he was still living, this Miracle Man would be celebrating his 117th birthday today.

January 03, 2009

D-I-N Ralph

Ralph roamed the streets of Reynolds as long as I can remember. The truth is I never knew his last name, and I'm not even sure Ralph was really his first name.

I suppose every small town has a Ralph.

Ralph always wore a heavy coat. If it was cold outside it came in handy. When it was 100 degrees he had to be miserable. But he always dressed like it was winter. He lived in an old shanty on the outside of town, but all he did was sleep there. When he wasn't sitting on a bench in town, he could be found walking along the roads and highways in the county. One night someone saw him walking down a highway 90 miles south of Reynolds. Some jerk had picked him up and taken him that far and put him out.

Some of us idiotic kids made fun of him. When we asked him how to spell "Ralph" he would quickly respond with these letters: D-I-N. He would say, "If you didn't know it then, you know it now."

He became known to many folks as D-I-N Ralph.

Ralph always had a harmonica packed away somewhere inside that coat. If you asked him to play it, he would proudly pull it out and begin playing. He would tap his foot and intermittently sing along with whatever he was playing. He would look in your eyes when he was playing and when he was done he would grin really big. He was not at all ashamed of his rotten teeth.

As I grew older I quit asking him to spell his name. I would give him a few dollars when I saw him. I picked him up in my truck when I passed him walking down the road. He always got in the back of the truck. I never remember him actually getting in the cab.

Ralph apparently never contributed much to society.

But maybe his contribution to society was not what God had in mind when he planted this Ralph in Reynolds.

Maybe it was about how folks like me would serve him and relate to him. Maybe this is what Jesus was talking about in *Matthew* 25:40 NIV.

The King will reply, 'I tell you the truth, whatever you did for one of the least of these brothers of mine, you did for me.

If so, I flunked the test.

God help me.

March 26, 2009

Simply Unforgettable

Sometimes we are fortunate enough to experience an unforgettable moment. I think my wife and I experienced one of those on Saturday afternoon. I know I can't do the moment justice here but it is worth giving it a try.

We were visiting my wife's mother in the assisted living facility yesterday afternoon and thought we heard someone playing the piano in one of the public rooms down the hall. We walked into the public room just in time to see an obviously distraught, cantankerous, irritated elderly lady trying to make her way out of the room using her walker. She was bent over and could hardly walk and seemed very confused. She was not talking very nicely to the nurse who had come in to try to help her.

She was not very interested in talking to us either, but I was curious to know if this was the lady who had been playing the piano. We coaxed her back to the piano bench. She told us she was from Louisiana but did not understand that she was in Georgia or how she got here. She did not know where her children live now and why they moved her to this facility. She didn't seem too happy about any of it.

Many of you reading this know what it's like to see a loved one begin having a difficult time remembering things. Many others also know what it's like when their mind gets to the point where they don't even remember or recognize their closest relatives. The time between when it all begins and when the mind completely goes can be a heart wrenching journey for a family.

It has to be a frightening journey for the person whose mind is slipping.

So we asked this frightened and confused elderly lady to play us something on the piano. She looked at us with a funny look on her face but turned to the piano and incredibly started playing. Not only was she playing beautifully, but she was also moving her head and body as if she was dancing with the music she was playing. It was obvious her music took her back to a safe place where life was normal and full of love and there was no fear of the unknown. Her music transformed her.

I have to tell you I sat in a chair and watched and listened with tears in my eyes when it dawned on me she was playing Nat King Cole's famous song, "Unforgettable."

Unforgettable, that's what you are

Unforgettable though near or far
Like a song of love that clings to me
How the thought of you does things to me
Never before has someone been more
Unforgettable in every way
And forever more, that's how you'll stay
That's why, darling, it's incredible
That someone so unforgettable
Thinks that I am unforgettable too.

My new friend Mrs. Ida went on to play a lot of songs for us. In fact, she could play every old song that we requested.

The truth is she will most likely not remember playing for us yesterday afternoon but she has not forgotten how to play the piano or the warm feeling her music brings to her.

Some things are simply unforgettable.

September 21, 2008

While There is Still Today

We have been visiting a local assisted living home on a regular basis, the last month or so since my mother-in-law became a resident. I have found myself on a few occasions sitting around the living room there visiting with some of the residents. Growing to an old age is a natural phenomenon that I hope I get to experience. The only option is growing dead. I'll take growing old.

I am intrigued with the conversations I've had with some of the residents. I think I am intrigued most with the human brain and how it works. Last night, we sat for at least an hour visiting with a very nice and obviously very educated elderly lady.

She explained that she would soon be 83 and had been a resident at that facility only since last Saturday.

She was concerned about whether they had already had Pavarotti's funeral. She went on to tell us that her mother actually heard the famous tenor Enrico Caruso in San Francisco in 1908. It was obvious her favorite tenor is Placido Domingo, and she shivered every time she mentioned his name.

She definitely had my curiosity up, and I discovered all kinds of things about this remarkable lady as I listened to her story. We heard all the very interesting details about her professional career as well as details about her beloved family and her church. She recalled detail after detail, and I was so impressed with her ability to remember so much at her age. After 45 minutes of conversation, my first clue that her memory was not perfect was when she could not remember the name of the book she was reading. A few minutes later she mentioned she was born in 1917. I immediately recognized that the birth date did not coincide with her almost 83 years of age she had told us earlier.

As we were leaving, Kathy and I discussed this remarkable lady and her incredible memory. I asked Kathy if she noticed that the lady either had her age or her birth date wrong. She did notice and out of curiosity we stopped by the office on the way out and asked the lady in the office how long this lady had been a resident there. We found out she had been there not since "last Saturday" as the lady had explained to us but she had been there over a month.

The human brain is an amazing thing. I have no idea how it works. For someone at that age to have such an outgoing personality, to be so well spoken, able to recall all the details of the past and even to know Pavarotti had died the day before and to seem to have "feelings" for another famous tenor was very impressive to say the least.

And then to discover she didn't know if she had been living in this facility for 6 days or a month and didn't know if she was 83 or 90 just caused me to be in awe.

Being in the funeral business, I have never lost focus that every day could be our last.

Last night, I was reminded that you don't have to die for that to happen. I left there with a new commitment to live every day to the fullest.

...while there is still today.

September 08, 2007

You Know the Tree by Its Fruit

(Oklahoma City) I met some new folks tonight at the Cheesecake Factory. Tim and Nona-Sue Mellish live in the OKC suburb of Bethany. Ellen Graham lives nearby in Yukon. I am somewhat familiar with both places since I visit this city quite often. I really don't know much about these very friendly folks except this one very important thing. They did a wonderful job raising their kids.

I found great pleasure in telling them just that tonight.

Their kids, by the way, are David and Jamie Graham who recently moved back to Oklahoma City from Warner Robins, Ga. Unlike most of the friends they made in Georgia, I promised them I would see them again.

I kept my promise.

When a young married couple moves all the way across the country from Oklahoma to Georgia where they know absolutely nobody, all their parents can do is hope and pray they raised them right. The parents will not be there to tell them who to hang out with or what to do with their time. All of a sudden they are on their own in a strange land where everything all of a sudden becomes permissible.

David and Jamie did it right the two years or so they were in Georgia. They joined a good church, got involved and made a lot of friends. They even hung out at our house from time to time with some of their friends. I knew somewhere there were parents who had done more than a few things right along the way. I was 100 percent correct.

I am the world's worst at remembering names. When we finished our meal and after a lot of conversation, I pulled out a piece of paper and asked the parents to give me their names again. David laughed and wondered what people at nearby tables were thinking. They had seen me join this group at their table. They watched us talk and laugh. And then they saw me pull out a piece of paper and ask for their names.

I did ask for their names, but I did not have to ask who they were. I already knew more about them than they realized.

Make no mistake about it. You know the tree by the fruit.

October 8, 2007

Things Sure Do Change

Some of my fondest memories when I was a kid are the sleepovers at the Montgomery farm in the Crowell Community outside of Reynolds. Stan Montgomery was my childhood friend and classmate. We would roam the woods and investigate whatever we happened to find. I remember even sleeping on top of a wagon full of cotton one night. I also remember a large bell in the yard that would be rung to let everybody know when lunch was ready. Being a "city" boy (I use that word very loosely), I had the opportunity to experience a way of life that was different and much fun.

On most of my weekend visits to Crowell, we would eventually visit Stan's grandparents. Actually both sets of his grandparents lived in the Crowell Community and really just down the road. You talk about a community made up of folks with generational relationships – Crowell was surely one of them.

I suppose because my focus was on playing with Stan at their farm and appreciating the fun at the moment, I was older before I really began to appreciate the wonderful way of life of folks like his grandparents, Lonnie and Sallie Mae Pierce. But I did see it. I guess you can say to some degree I tasted it.

Sometimes I wish I could, as an adult, go back in time for just one day and sit under that big ole pecan tree in the Pierce's yard and have a long chat with them about their simple life. Maybe we could shell some butterbeans as we chat. Or maybe I could get Mr. Lonnie to teach me how to peel a peach in one piece without breaking the peel. Better than that, maybe we could sit around the table as we talk and partake of the feast that was always on that table. And before I was transplanted back to 2009, I would have to have a piece of Miss Sallie Mae's fresh 'nanna pudding that always seemed to be in a bowl big enough to look like it was meant for the school cafeteria. Somehow I would have to save room for a bite of her blackberry pie and maybe a couple of bites of her famous strawberry shortcake.

I can tell you I would leave very full from the abundance of freshly cooked farm food and over the top southern hospitality. I would also leave with much more wisdom than I have today.

To give you a little background, Lonnie Pierce was born a few years before the turn of the twentieth century. His wife, sweetheart, soul mate and best friend, Sallie Mae, was a few years younger. They produced five incredible children-- four are still living--and had a wonderful life together for 60 years.

I know all their children and I am quite certain they are among the richest folks I know. The currency deposited in their accounts by their parents that made them so rich had nothing to do with money, although to my knowledge none of them have ever wanted for anything. But the currency consisted of much more important things such as hard work, honesty, integrity, selflessness, politeness, more hard work, laughter, commitment to God, commitment to the local church, commitment to the community, lovers of the land and soil, more hard work, close knit family, common sense, humility and more graciousness that you can shake a stick at.

They were simply made out of special fabric.

Mr. Lonnie never got sick or maybe he just refused to get sick. If he was feeling bad, he would take a dose of mineral oil and keep going. He worked from early morning to sundown. One of the greatest compliments paid to him was from one of his former farm hands who said, "Mr. Lonnie was the hardest working man I ever knew."

But in spite of the relentless hard work--if you caught his eye, this man who did not have a curse word in his vocabulary, would raise his sweat stained straw hat to you.

The children remember the special treatment for their feet when they were cut from playing barefooted. Their mom would wash their feet in kerosene. The pain would increase but the healing would begin. They also remember the remedy for a dog getting bit by a rattlesnake. Take a tablespoon of cracked alum and mix it with two egg yellows and pour it down the dog's throat. Both treatments worked very well, thank you.

Sallie Mae not only taught her girls to cook but also to sew… and fish. Chicken feed sacks made perfect dresses. And just because it started to rain didn't mean it was time to stop fishing.

They grew whopper watermelons, the best tasting tomatoes, huge turnip roots, butter beans, squash and just keep naming. They drank milk from their own cows, ate their own chickens and ate sausage and bacon from their own hogs. They also shared the fruits of their labor with their neighbors. In fact, Sallie Mae was not only quick to share her vegetables, but she was known to delight in delivering butter beans to her neighbors - shelled, washed and ready to cook.

Sallie Mae suffered from asthma most all her life. One of the sons remembers leaving for school one morning and wondering if his mom would be alive when he got home because of the difficulty she was having breathing. He kneeled by a light pole on that particular morning facing the east and prayed that God would make his mama better. As a young boy, he saw a vision in the eastern sky as he bowed to pray that morning. When he got home that afternoon she was feeling great and was like a new person. He has been a believer ever since.

After all the kids were grown and married, they decided to pool their money and build their parents an inside bathroom. The children and their spouses came to the house to see the finished product and celebrate the occasion. When one son-in-law and his wife drove up that afternoon, Mr. Lonnie and his three sons were in the back yard cooking fish in a new Coleman cooker using the tailgate of his pickup truck as a table.

Mr. Lonnie greeted his son-in-law with this comment, "You know 'Billam,' we raised five wonderful children in this house, and we're proud of each one. We cooked inside and went to the outhouse outside - now, here I am cooking outside and now we go to the toilet inside - things sure do change, don't they?"

Things sure do change.

But Lonnie and Sallie Mae Pierce and their family did just fine before they did.

January 21, 2009

Southern Roots

I'm not exactly sure of the year, but sometime in the early seventies Gary Oliver from Oxford N.Y. made his first trip to Reynolds. He has made a ton of trips since that day. He came to Reynolds to spend the weekend and to meet the parents of his girlfriend, Nancy Whatley. Both Nancy and Gary were students at the University of Georgia.

Nancy's parents, Ed and Rosemary Whatley, had to attend a function out of town that Friday night on his first trip, and they asked my dad and mom who lived next door to welcome Gary to Reynolds and make him feel at home until they could get back that night. That was definitely right up my daddy and mama's alley.

I don't think Gary had ever met anyone quite like my dad. Daddy loved the fact he was from New York and had a different accent so Gary got the full treatment. And since my dad was an avid golfer, he also loved the fact that Gary played on the University of Georgia golf team. They hit it off quickly and became great friends.

Gary and Nancy also hit it off as well and got married a couple or so years later.

One of the groomsmen who was supposed to be in their wedding had an emergency at the last minute and could not make it to the wedding. Being the good neighbor, I took his place. Not only did I take Gary's friend's place at the wedding, but I also took his place at the bachelor's party the night before.

Trying to exhibit the best southern hospitality possible, the groomsmen took Gary to the outskirts of town the night before the wedding and took his clothes off and left him on a dirt road. Of course, we told the night policeman what we were doing and asked him to join in our little prank. So when Gary's buck naked self came sneaking back into town in an attempt to get back to the Whatley's house, the policeman picked him up for indecent exposure. We were across the street from the City Hall when Gary was taken out of the back of the police car with a sheet (provided by the policeman) wrapped around him. Gary, not knowing the policeman was in on our prank, was trying to explain to the policeman that he was marrying Dr. Whatley's daughter and his friends did this to him for his bachelor's party. We heard the policeman reply, "I don't know a Dr. Whatley."

We laughed but Gary got the next laugh.

About 4 AM, I was awakened by a bucket of cold water being poured on my face. I was asleep on the sofa in my Mama's formal living room. Gary could not have cared less at that point if he ruined the sofa or not. It would be safe to say I woke up rather quickly.

Gary, being the good natured fellow he is, took it all in stride. But after he broke out from head to toe with poison ivy on their honeymoon, I did make sure he was not invited to my bachelor's party a few years later. I have no doubt that Gary would have gone to great lengths to see if I was as good natured as he had been a few years earlier.

After Gary moved from Oxford, N.Y. to attend the University of Georgia, he never went back home. Of course, he visited from time to time but he quickly settled in the South and blended right in with the rest of us.

In a few weeks Gary and Nancy are scheduled to enter the ranks of the grandparent club.

And Gary's southern roots will run as deep as they can get.

May 2, 2008

You Might Be Surprised

(Chicago) I had an unusual 45 minutes or so in what I thought would be a normal cab ride last night from O'Hare Airport to a downtown hotel here.

I struck up a conversation with the cab driver. After a few minutes of conversing in our very different dialects, he asked me why I was in town. I told him I was here to speak at a conference. He asked me what subject I spoke about.

So I told him and gave him my view on life and told him a few of my stories from the perspective of a small town undertaker. He was listening and then began asking me questions. Before I knew it, he was telling me his life story. The cab driver told me about his mother who paid attention to him as a kid only when he was in trouble. He explained to me that he did not have good role models when he was growing up. He told me he now had a family of his own and how difficult it is to balance driving a cab and spending time and providing for his family. He said he could not give them all they needed. It was an emotional conversation and amazingly he poured his heart out to this perfect stranger in his cab. I have to tell you when we pulled up at the hotel last night I hated to get out of the car. I had this thought that I would never see this cab driver with tears in his eyes again. And I'm sure I won't.

But for 45 minutes I gave him my best shot. I have no doubt he appreciated the 45 minutes we had. I got the feeling our heartfelt conversation was a bright spot in his day yesterday ... and maybe his week or month. And maybe even his life.

A few weeks ago I was on a plane and was talking with a guy sitting next to me. A lady in front of us, who happened to be an anesthesiologist, turned around and joined in the conversation. I got both their addresses before I left the plane and sent them both a copy of my book, *View From A Hearse,* a few days later when I got back home. Last week, I got a note from one of my new friends. She told me how much she enjoyed the book and went on to say meeting me and reading my book was a blessing because just before meeting me her fiancé had been killed in a tragic accident.

The point is you never know what the people we meet by chance every day are going through. But then again maybe the meetings are not by chance. Maybe in the big scheme of things encounters like these are orchestrated. A God who put the stars in the sky and orchestrated the universe could certainly put people in the right place at the right time.

But the truth is, we probably miss most of opportunities because it is easier for us to just keep to ourselves and avoid the people God puts in our path. Or maybe we feel we don't have anything to offer.

The truth is anybody can offer a word of encouragement. I am convinced people don't need a lecture or a well intended lesson on living life. They just need a real life story and a listening ear. Everybody has real- life stories they can share that have the potential to touch another person and give hope to someone who has lost theirs.

Keep your eyes and ears open and live by intention. You might be surprised at what you find. And the blessings you get in the process.

April 10, 2008

Rabbi Toms is the Real Deal

I'll never forget one Labor Day morning years ago, I got a call from a lady wanting to know if I had Mr. Smith (name is changed to protect the innocent) at the funeral home. I told the lady I did not. She quickly stated that she was just checking because she had heard he was not expected to make it through the telethon. I hung up the phone, and I was scratching my head wondering what in the world she was talking about. It dawned on me she was talking about the Jerry Lewis Telethon. It was not only a 24 hour telecast, but it had become the pivotal gauge of how long someone might live. I was impressed.

But these days, I think of someone else when Labor Day and the MDA Telethon shows up on television. For the past few years, a local firefighter by the name of Randy Toms is one of the local celebrity television hosts who uses his gift of gab and passion for the cause to raise funds for this very worthy charity. I make it a point to watch a few of the segments when he is on just to watch him work. In fact last Sunday night, my wife and I attended a gospel benefit for MDA held at our church sponsored by the Warner Robins Fire Department. Randy Toms was the Master of Ceremonies. He was funny, and he was passionate. I really don't know of anyone who could have done it better.

For the record, Randy Toms (I call him Rabbi) was my Sunday School teacher for a couple of years. To be honest, I've sat through and taught enough boring Sunday school classes to last me a lifetime. Sometimes those forty-five minute classes can be brutal early on a Sunday morning. But every now and then you run into a gifted teacher. Rabbi Toms is one of the gifted ones. The forty-five minutes in his class felt like five minutes, and the teacher was anything but boring.

Randy has other credentials. He punted way past his coverage on his wedding day and landed a beautiful wife. Randy and Jane have two grown children and a daughter-in-law. They are a great looking family, and it is very obvious they did something very right in raising their kids.

Randy is also the Chaplain of the Georgia Association of Fire Chiefs and has recently founded a ministry called the "Georgia Public Safety Ministries, Inc." Randy says that "public safety workers are always the first called in times of need but all too often the needs of the public safety workers go unmet.

The emergency services (fire, EMS and law enforcement) consistently have the highest rate of divorce, suicide and substance abuse of any profession."

Through his ministry, Randy speaks not only to fire departments and other emergency service groups around the state but also to churches and community groups. His desire is not only to help emergency workers in all facets of their lives, but he also has a vision of helping churches and communities to "reach beyond what is normal and serve their public servants."

Randy "Rabbi" Toms is the real deal.

And I have seen a few deals in my life.

August 03, 2007

Way Too Often These Days

A few days ago when I was going in and out of the Houston County Medical Center as much as possible to see my new grandbaby, I ran into an old friend from home standing at the front door.

I asked him what he was doing at the hospital. Ricky told me his Uncle Jack had broken his hip and was not doing well at all. He told me he was worried about him. I got his room number and told Ricky I would drop by to see him.

Jack Hobbs has lived all his life in a "suburb" of Reynolds called Hobbsville. You won't find Hobbsville on a map because the Hobbsville sign was erected by the Hobbs family, not by the State of Georgia. Several generations of Hobbs have lived in this little community. Jack's brother, Snook, and his cousin GC raised their families there. Snook and GC both had a house full of children. Jack never got married.

This "bachelor" uncle has always been loved and looked after by his many nephews and nieces who live near him. I was not surprised that a couple of them were at his side at the hospital last week.

Jack has lived a simple life. He bought a brand new pick up truck in 1968 and was still driving until recently when his family made him quit driving. Not many people drive the same vehicle for 37 years. Jack never worried about impressing anybody. He just lived his life and tended to his own business.

I really don't think Jack was worried about how much he owed on his credit card when he was admitted in the hospital. I've never checked his credit report, but I have a strong feeling he doesn't have a credit report. He paid cash for whatever he bought.

One can learn a lot about living from a man like Jack Hobbs. I was always impressed by the way Jack lived his life.

I got to know him at visitations at the funeral home through my dad when I was a young kid. Jack and my dad were in the same class in school and they were big buddies. Jack never liked the idea of being around dead people. He never could understand how we did it. But he and daddy always had a story to tell about something that happened 50 years ago. He was one of those people you just loved being around.

As I did with many of my dad's friends, I also became friends with Jack.

We had our own stories to tell after many years of knowing each other.

I realized as I entered the elevator to go up to his room the other day that I had not seen Jack in a few years. When I walked in his room and saw him, I realized he didn't look good at all. I didn't know if he was cognizant of what was going on or not. The family members who were in the room told me to speak to him, but they had no idea if he would respond or not.

I stood over him and said loud enough for him to hear me, "Mr. Jack Hobbs, do you know who this is?"

I heard a grunt but no answer.

I then said, "This is your ole buddy, Bruce Goddard."

Without opening his eyes he responded with a smile, "I don't think I want to be seeing an undertaker right now."

"Jack at least you are talking to him," was my response.

We all laughed. And Jack smiled wider.

We visited for a few minutes, but I left there with an empty feeling in my stomach. I'm at the age now where people I knew so well and who influenced me in so many ways are dying way too often.

There are a lot of neat things about being in my fifties.

But watching my friends die is not one of them.

January 30, 2007

Bryant the Shoeshine Man

Let me introduce you to my friend Bryant the shoeshine man. He has shined my shoes numerous times at Hartsfield – Jackson International Airport.

In fact, this 67 year old man has been shining a lot of people's shoes for the past 47 years. He now works from noon to 7p.m. and works only five days a week. He has slowed down, but he is not planning on stopping. Bryant tells me that he will shine shoes until he can't do it anymore. From the way he was working today, I would guess the retirement date is not in the immediate future.

Based on the information he gave me today and doing a little quick math in my head, Bryant has shined somewhere close to 200,000 pairs of shoes in his career. And is still counting.

When I asked him how many famous people have been his customer over the years, Bryant told me he doesn't shine the shoes of celebrities very often these days. He said most of the time they don't enter through the main terminal anymore. He reluctantly told me that he shined Dr. Martin Luther King's shoes a few times as he and his entourage came through the airport years ago. But I did not get the idea that he was very impressed.

In fact, I got the idea that not many people impress Bryant. I would suppose if I had been shining shoes for 47 years not many people would impress me either.

But then, he told me about his wife of 49 years who is now retired, and he told me about his two grown daughters. When he talked about them, he stopped shining, stood up and looked me in the eye. I could see his pride.

When he finished and I got up, I shook his hand and looked him in the eye. I thanked him for his life of hard work and the example I am certain he has set for his family and others. In America where many people live off the taxpayer's money and think somehow the rest of us owe them a living, Bryant has never had that mentality. He has earned his way with hard work, plenty of sweat and I'm sure some tears along the way.

I can tell you my Johnston & Murphy shoes didn't impress Bryant one bit today.

But Bryant, the shoeshine man, sure impressed me.

May 01, 2007

She Never Charged a Dime

I called her "Miss" Rachel. She was my friend, and I know she loved me, and I loved her. If she told me one time – she told me a hundred times: "I want you to speak at my funeral when I die." I never said I would because I always told her she could speak at my funeral because she was going to outlive me. She would always look at me with that "look" with her hands on her hips as if she was about to slap me – and then she would flash that great big smile.

I don't remember the first time I met "Miss" Rachel. I suppose I've known her all my life. I do remember she made my "groom's" cake when I got married 28 years ago. I remember her being a loyal customer at our grocery store, and I remember my visits with her at the doctor's office when she worked there. I also remember she was almost always in the audience when I was invited to speak at different churches in the county.

But where I really got to know "Miss" Rachel was in the most unusual place of all…the preparation room at the funeral home. There would usually be only three of us in the room: "Miss" Rachael, me and the lady lying on the table whose hair she was fixin'. Miss Rachael and I did all the talking (thank goodness). The hair fixin' would have ended really quickly if the person lying on the table had spoken.

There is no telling how many hairdos she fixed in that back room at the funeral home preparing someone for burial. She knew most of those people, but some she did not know. There is no doubt she holds the record at Goddard Funeral Home, at least for the last 30 years. She always would come whenever I called. Sometimes she would say, "I've to get this cake out of the oven first," but she always came--no matter what time of the day or night or what day of the week.

I would always be sure her water bottle and curlers were in the right place because if they weren't, she would be quick to let me know.

She never charged one dime. I tried to pay her. She always refused. I can still hear her saying, "This is the last thing I can do for them."

Sometimes I would say, "Miss Rachel, you don't even know this lady!"

She would always respond, "Don't matter. I'm not taking your money."

I finally gave up.

I don't remember much about the hair she was fixin.' But I do remember many of the conversations we had, and to be honest, I lived through many of her trials with her. I remember when her mom died and I had the privilege of walking through that with her. She trusted me and she would share her innermost thoughts and heart with me. I remember her concerns about personal family conflicts. I remember the load she carried taking care of her husband after he got ill. I also remember her concern about the spiritual welfare of some of her family and friends. I remember a lot of tears, and I remember a lot of laughter.

She was always focusing on the needs of others and she took joy in that. She had a servant's heart and considered the needs of others more important than her own.

In my view, there are two types of people in the world. There are the givers and there are the takers. Rachel Wainwright was a giver. No doubt about that.

Sunday afternoon, I walked through the back door of the funeral home when the funeral director was just about to place her body in the casket. I suddenly found myself in that very familiar room with this very familiar lady. I asked him to let me help. So I had the privilege to help place her body into the casket.

I think Miss Rachel would have liked that.

She would not have liked it that I told you about the fact she wouldn't charge for doing hair. She always said if she got rewarded on earth for her good deeds she would miss the reward in heaven.

Since she already received the heavenly reward, I hope she will forgive me.

August 30, 2006

The Greatest Generation

(Reynolds, Ga.) Everybody should have had the privilege of growing up in a small town. As I have said many times, I wouldn't take a million dollars for growing up in Reynolds.

I went back home today and got to see some folks I haven't seen in a long time. These people are not just acquaintances. They are lifelong friends, and as I have mentioned before, the friendships are generational. These folks are family to me.

I was there not under the best of circumstances. I was in town to speak at a funeral. I don't remember when I first met Ted Parks. I've known him all my life. It was an honor to be asked to speak at his funeral service at the First Baptist Church today.

Ted Parks was a very big man. He was big physically, and he was also big in many other ways.

He left Reynolds as a teenager many years ago because he wanted to make sure he got his high school education. His parents believed in hard work and made sure their children worked in the fields. Ted knew if he stayed at home he would either have to drop out of school because of the work required of him or he would fall behind in his studies and be in a position to fail.

He moved 40 miles away to Macon to live with his older brother. To support himself, he got a job at a laundry. He attended a much larger high school there and started playing football. He was a good enough football player to be offered a scholarship at the University of Georgia when he graduated. He did play for the Bulldogs and should have been a member of the 1943 Bulldog team that played UCLA in the Rose Bowl. He had enlisted in the US Navy and was in the South Pacific when his teammates were preparing for that game.

When he returned from the war, he continued his college education at Mercer University. He played football there and had an invitation to play pro ball by two teams but turned them down because there was not enough money in it, and he had already started a family. He got a degree in Economics at Mercer and had a minor in Physical Education.

He lived in Reynolds all his working life and spent his entire career working at a nearby Air Force Base as a civilian employee. He also farmed on the side.

When Ted was a young man, he was the person the county called upon when someone drowned. He would be called upon to dive to the bottom of the river or ponds in the county to pull a body from the bottom. Today people wear wet suits and air tanks and go through a lot of training to do such. Ted did it on sheer athletic ability with no training.

Ted also was a musician. He played a pretty mean guitar and also played the harmonica. His wife remembers him singing to her many times during their younger married days.

On many occasions during my adult life in Reynolds, I sat at a breakfast table with Ted and some of his buddies and drank coffee and listened to the stories. He was plain spoken and very opinionated. He was one of the most interesting people I ever talked to in my life. Sometimes he would be funny when he was not trying to be funny and sometimes he would be funny with a purpose.

He was big enough and strong enough to never have to back down from anyone. But his heart was tender enough for him to be moved to tears when the discussion came to his family, his country, priorities and spiritual truths.

He didn't drink or smoke. He would tell you in a heartbeat that he hated a drunk. But some of his favorite people in the world were people who had problems with alcohol.

That says almost everything you need to know about Ted Parks.

Another thing you should know is that he and his wife, Mattie, celebrated their 63rd wedding anniversary a week before he died. That says almost everything else you need to know.

I spoke to his oldest daughter yesterday morning.

She said all the rest you need to know about her dad in one simple sentence.

"He was my hero."

And the other two children echo her sentiments.

As I drove out of Reynolds today I had one thing on my mind. You just don't see many people like Ted Parks anymore. Another member of the "Greatest Generation" who helped pave the way for the rest of us has passed away.

And, I just don't think we are replacing folks like that.

December 17, 2006

He Made It Home

I got another one of those calls this morning that caused me to stop in my tracks. I was traveling in Mississippi when the call came. When I saw the caller ID and realized the caller was David McLeighton, I knew somebody had passed away. David is now the owner and operator of Goddard Funeral Home. As you certainly know, I have roots and connections in the service area of Goddard Funeral Home that are very deep and long lasting.

So I just held my breath as I answered my cell phone. David quickly told me Rannie Gaultney was found dead this morning. This preacher man who I called "The Right Reverend" was my friend. We spent many hours together from the middle seventies to the late eighties.

I swallowed hard.

He began working at our funeral home with my dad and my brother when I was at UGA. When I came back from college and mortuary school and began running the funeral home in Reynolds, Rannie was there. For a period of about 12 years he made almost every death call with me and worked every funeral with me.

We traveled many hours and miles together at all hours of the night. We discussed every subject that could possibly be discussed.

At an early age, Rannie was called to be a preacher, and he never wavered from that call on his life. He was always prepared to preach in season and out of season. If anyone has ever been faithful to the call on his life it was Rannie Gaultney.

After I graduated from mortuary school, I gave all my books and study materials to Rannie, so he could take the test to become a licensed Funeral Director. I even tutored him while he was studying, since I had just come out of mortuary school and the material was still fresh on my mind. He took the test, and he passed. He was in the last group who was able to get a license in Georgia without attending mortuary school.

The State Board of Funeral Services changed the rules after that year. Rannie was proud when he got that license. I was proud for him.

The Right Reverend Gaultney was a Baptist preacher who turned charismatic. He left the main stream Baptist church and started a new church that met in his home. That growing church eventually moved to a store front building and finally built a church building.

I knew him when he was Baptist, and I knew him when he was charismatic. Although he was misunderstood by some, I always understood him.

He was considered as somewhat controversial because his members came from the main stream churches from around the county, and the other churches didn't like losing their members.

He was also controversial because he never minced his words. He always said what he thought whether in the pulpit or out of the pulpit. Sometimes that got him in trouble, but he didn't have a "politically correct" bone in his body. He never preached what his hearer's "itching ears" wanted to hear.

People either loved him or they left him alone.

I loved him.

His "not mincing" his words had a major impact on my life at a very crucial time in my life when I needed some plainly spoken words. That impact was during the time when I just came out of college and was about to begin this thing called life in the real world. I had questions, and I was searching for answers.

He was not bashful about providing those answers as he knew them.

He told me many times in later years that he wanted me to speak at his funeral service when he died. I got a call this afternoon asking me to do that.

If I'm breathing, I will be there.

It is a sad day for his family, his church members and all the rest of us he is leaving behind. But for him, it is the day he has looked to and preached about for most of his life.

He has fought the good fight. He has finished the race. He has kept the faith.

Now there is in store for him the crown of righteousness.

The Right Reverend Rannie Gaultney has made it home.

February 21, 2007

There Will Never Be Another Karona

Karona (pronounced Kayroni) Wainwright was an institution in Taylor County, Georgia. When God made him He threw away the mold. There will never be another like him.

All he needed was an agent and he could have had his own sitcom on national TV. If you can get a mental picture of Squeeky on *Laverne and Shirley,* that TV character was Karona in real life.

He always had a joke. When Karona walked up to me, I was always looking both ways to see who was listening. He would say anything.

Karona spent most of his time trapping and/or hunting. His normal attire was camouflage. I'm sure he had other clothes but he never wore them. A normal scene in Reynolds was to see several people gathered around the back of Karona's pick-up truck to see what kind of varmint he had conquered.

For several years, I traveled to every corner of rural Georgia speaking at almost every civic club and organization you can imagine. I always asked people if they had heard of Reynolds.

Most of the time there would be three reasons people had heard of Reynolds. One was Garland Byrd, who was a former Lt. Governor of the state. Everybody knew him. The second was the Silver Dollar Raceway. I think there are people in every county in the state who has raced at Ed Swearingen's raceway.

The third was Karona Wainwright. It was amazing how many people throughout the state knew Karona. They always had a funny story to tell about him.

I could never forget the comment Karona made during the funeral procession at his grandmother's funeral. He was sitting in the back seat between his mother and his aunt. They were visibly upset and crying, Karona had his arm around both of them. Out of the clear blue he asked me if I knew how many people it took to eat a possum.

The crying stopped and it got silent in the car so I figured I needed to answer him.

"No, Karona," I answered. "How many?"

Since it's not cool for an undertaker to laugh during a funeral, his reply almost caused me to bend the steering wheel to keep from it.

"Three. Two to watch the traffic," was his reply.

He put his arms back around his mother and aunt … and the mourning continued. I can tell you there was nothing his mother and aunt could do with him. They didn't even try.

Karona suffered a heart attack a few years ago and was rushed by ambulance to a nearby hospital where he was admitted into their ICU. They scheduled some tests for the next day, so the doctors could understand the extent of the damage to his heart.

Karona promptly checked himself out of the hospital. He told the doctors he had to get back to Taylor County. Deer season opened the next day, and he couldn't miss it.

He collapsed the next morning before he could get into his stand. He was rushed back to the hospital, but this time he didn't make it.

I was honored to be asked to speak at his funeral service, and we celebrated his life just as it was. I remember there was laughter and tears that day. We had to laugh as we remembered some of the stories that made him so unique. We had to cry because we knew he left us much too soon.

There will never be another Karona Wainwright.

And I carry a piece of him wherever I go.

August 21, 2006

Tough as Nails

Pat Patterson moved to Reynolds with the railroad. I have forgotten all the positions he had over the years while with the railroad, but I do know he managed the depot in Reynolds and worked for the railroad all his life until he retired.

The Patterson family lived right up the street from me when I was a kid. My brother and I played with Billy and Cal up and down the streets of Reynolds as we were growing up. We are lifelong friends.

Janet, Pat's wife and Billy and Cal's mom, has always been a special friend to me. She and my mom were friends for years.

I remember being sad when the Pattersons moved away. They really didn't move that far. Only two streets over.

They moved in a new house next to the ball diamond. It actually worked out really good to have somewhere to go when it started raining when we were playing ball, but it was tough for me when they moved.

Pat Patterson passed away last year. The Pattersons asked me to speak at his funeral service. I was honored to do it, and it caused me to stop and think about some pretty important stuff.

Pat (I called him Mr. Pat by the way) was a tough guy. He was strong as an ox and never had a bit of trouble telling you what he thought about whatever subject that happened to be on the table.

I remember he was umpiring a church softball game one night and one of the leaders in a particular church got mad at a call he made at second base and temporarily lost his Christianity. He got in Mr. Pat's face to express his displeasure.

I thought Mr. Pat was going to tear him apart. The church leader got in the wrong man's face. He almost lost his church membership permanently, because I thought Mr. Pat was going to rip his head off.

As a kid, I saw all that but I also saw another side to this tough man.

He was my little league coach. And at a very important time of my life he made me feel like I was the best ballplayer east of Mississippi. I remember he bragged on me to others when I didn't think he knew I could hear. As I got older, I realized he knew I could hear all along.

He was motivating me to make me better.

Not only in baseball.

But also in life, and he was very good at doing that.

I smiled years later when I was standing with him watching his grandson, Brad, play high school ball. Brad was playing first base and a pop fly was hit into the infield. As Brad was looking up and reaching up to catch the ball, the runner ran him over. It was a cheap shot while Brad was defenseless, and I thought Mr. Pat was going to go through the fence. He was ready to whip the boy and his parents and grandparents.

I smiled because he was still tough as they come, and he still would not back down from anybody even as a senior adult. He was mad as rip, and I was afraid he would have a heart attack that day.

But the neat thing to me was that he just loved his grandson and he wanted to protect him. He knew the rules of baseball, and it was a cheap shot. Billy and Cal had to calm him down that day.

But I left that game reminded of my appreciation for him and being thankful for the impact he had in my life for so many years.

Somehow in the big scheme of things God just puts people in your life for the purpose of helping you become whoever He wants you to become.

I have no doubt that Pat Patterson was one of those people.

The truth is he probably never knew the impact he had on me.

I did get to tell his family and all the friends who gathered for that funeral that day. But I never told him.

I wish I had.

He was tough as nails.

But he had a heart of gold.

September 19, 2006

To Touch a Company

(Houston, Texas) Having been self employed all my life, I suddenly found myself working for someone else for the first time in my career in 1997. Although I continued to run my funeral homes (along with a few others) and was continuing to serve families I had known all my life, I found myself in an unfamiliar and somewhat uncomfortable situation.

You just don't take a small town country boy and throw him into the waters of a large publically traded company without some struggles for the country boy along the way.

When I look back, I had no idea of the career opportunity this move would eventually afford me. I certainly had no idea of the opportunity I would have to become friends with folks from different parts of the country who would change my life.

Not long after I had sold my businesses, I received a call from a man from New York City. I have to tell you in those days New York City seemed like a long way from Reynolds. I was in my office one day and found myself not only talking to a man a long way away but also one who talked a little differently than me.

Actually that would be a lot differently.

He was questioning me about a decision I had made about a casket I had ordered. I could not understand how a man from NYC would care about my casket order. To be honest, after running my businesses all my life to that point, I didn't think I needed assistance from someone in NYC regarding what casket I needed to order. After a lengthy conversation, I told him exactly what I thought.

I would find out later that John Roefaro had a huge job in our company as head of revenue services for the Eastern United States. I would meet John a few weeks after our phone conversation in Houston at a training school. John was one of the facilitators of my training. I was smart enough to know I needed to introduce myself to him and make amends for our previous conversation.

But before I could do that, John introduced himself to me.

He told me had heard I was a humorist. Then John began to tell me one joke after another. As you might imagine, I had a few of my own as well. Before we knew it, we both were laughing, and I mean really laughing.

And in just a few short minutes, this stranger who had made me feel so uncomfortable a few weeks earlier had made me feel very comfortable.

Over the past 12 years, John and I have not only been co-workers but more importantly we have become friends. For a man who I didn't think had much to offer me during our first encounter over the telephone, he has taught me much and has been a mentor to me.

I could talk about John's experience, his presentation skills, his leadership skills, his humor, his integrity and many other traits and attributes I have come to appreciate about him over the years.

But the greatest lesson I have learned is about the distance from Reynolds to New York City. It is not nearly as great as I once thought.

By the way, John is celebrating his 40th year with our company this year, and yesterday he was honored by the officers of our company for his outstanding career. I can tell you I was glad I was there and able to witness the presentation.

"Most of us have had the opportunity to touch some folks," someone said, "but John has an opportunity to touch a company."

I can tell you I am glad to be a part of the company he keeps... and touches.

May 21, 2009

Chill Bump Moment

Growing up in the funeral business in a small town, I knew most everybody we buried. Further, I have many memories in this head of mine about certain funerals. If you have read my book, *View From a Hearse*, you know some of the funniest things happen at the most serious times. A funeral, being a serious time, can produce some funny moments, which is the subject of the other book.

But there have been many more moments that had nothing to do with funny. Some of those memories, I will take with me to the grave. Emotional moments. Chill bump moments. One of those emotional, chill bump moments I will always remember was the day we buried Sydney Bryan.

Sydney Bryan was the son of the man who served as the town doctor for many years. While Sydney was the only one of Dr. Bryan's children who elected to stay in Reynolds, his siblings and their families visited often. Sydney's brother and sisters obviously had Reynolds roots and many friends in Reynolds but their children were just as well known in Reynolds. Each summer when they came to town, they would pick right up where they left off last time. If local kids were having birthday parties, swimming parties or backyard parties they would always be invited. The Bryan's were known for large family gatherings that took place in a large two story house known as "Big House" that stood across from the First Baptist Church. The gatherings centered around a huge dining room table with enormous amounts of real southern food. There is no doubt that those nieces and nephews have many fond memories of those visits to Reynolds. "Big House" was the epitome of the good life in the South.

The truth is Sydney Bryan was the epitome of the Southern gentleman. There is no telling how much he gave away to his workers in the fields or to others who were struggling or to others just to be nice. I vividly remember many afternoons seeing several bunches of turnip greens or a basket of peaches at my parent's back door that Sydney left. He was a farmer and made his living on the land. He never minded sharing the fruits of his labor.

Sydney was also an avid outdoorsman who spent a ton of hours in the woods and in the swamp. He appreciated and understood God's creation as much as anyone I ever met. He enjoyed teaching others to hunt and fish as much as he enjoyed hunting and fishing himself. If someone called a meeting for everyone Sydney Bryan taught to hunt and fish, I can tell you there would be a large very appreciative crowd gathered for that meeting.

More than anything Sydney was proud to be a Southerner. Contrary to what many believe who do not have Southern roots, Sydney's southern pride had nothing to do with racism or hatred. It had to do with a wonderful way of life in which he enjoyed to the fullest. I have learned as I have traveled around our great country that there are some who have a stereotypical mindset toward people who live in the South. There are others who have friends in the South or have visited who know better. The South and the life it represents has been feared, revered, hated and loved. For those of us who have southern roots, the revered and loved applies. Sydney Bryan revered the South. He loved his family he loved his country and he loved the South.

There was a huge crowd gathered at the First Baptist Church of Reynolds for Sydney Bryan's funeral on that spring day in 1993. The church was packed. We had speakers set up for the overflow crowd who were seated in the packed fellowship hall in the back. Additionally, there were as many people standing on the lawn outside as were seated inside. I was thinking that day that this southern gentleman had impacted an awful lot of folks.

Terry McDaniel, who was Reynolds' female answer to Liberace, was playing the piano that day. Believe me, she was "walking all over it" as we say in the South. When the service was over, my team walked down front to dismiss the family and friends and to roll the casket out down the center aisle of the church. As the casket began to roll, Terry began to change the song she was playing on the piano. When I realized what she was playing, I stopped in my tracks. The words to the song she was playing were running through my mind.It was one of those "chill bump" moments I will never forget.

I wish I was in the land of cotton
Old times there are not forgotten
Look away look away look away Dixie Land.
In Dixie Land I'll take my stand
To live and die in Dixie.
Away, away, away down South in Dixie.

Today, I live and work with people from all over our country. I have learned that people are the same wherever you go. Some of my closest friends have never lived in the South and that is certainly just fine. But I am proud to be a Southerner. When someone questions my "southernness," I always remember that chill bump moment at the First Baptist Church of Reynolds.

I was not one of those that Sydney Bryan taught to hunt and fish. But he did teach me in his life and in his death to never back down from being proud of my Southern roots.

I haven't. And I never will.

June 17, 2007

Simply an Angel

(Cabo San Lucas, Mexico) This morning about 3 a.m. Cabo time and about 5 a.m. Georgia, USA time my blackberry started vibrating. I have a strong feeling that heaven started vibrating about 30 minutes earlier when Jessie Mae King, P.O. Box 1, Reynolds Georgia, made her grand appearance.

I'm not sure how they do it in heaven, but I am quite positive a huge celebration began there this morning. I can picture the heavenly choir gathered, and the trumpets sounding louder than maybe they have ever sounded. Maybe the door swung open, and the huge throng of saints from ages past stood on their feet with loud applause as Jessie Mae King was escorted down the aisle. If my mom and dad were not escorting her, I am positive they were very close by.

Jessie Mae King was escorted down to the front row. I know that because my daddy always told me that Jessie may not have had a lot of riches on earth but she would be on the front row in heaven. If I heard that one time, I heard it a thousand times. So I know she is on the front row. And if they hand out rewards in heaven, she is having a difficult time counting them all today.

For many years Jessie wore "hand-me-down" clothes. Today, she is clothed with majesty. For many years she and her family lived in a one room home. Today, she is walking around an indescribable mansion that was prepared for her before the beginning of time.

For most of her life she cooked and cleaned house and help raise other folks' children. I was one of those children, and so were my children. The Jesus she talked about in almost every sentence that came out of her mouth has looked at her in the eye and said those words that she has been longing to hear: "Well done thy good and faithful servant."

I think of her every single time I hear the story of Jesus washing his disciple's feet.

I am reminded that the evidence of love is humility.

For the record, next to my parents, Jessie Mae King impacted my life more than any person I have ever known. She led a very simple life, but one of the most profound I have ever known. She was simply an angel.

I have no idea where I would be if not for this angel.

My loss is heaven's gain.

October 27, 2007

Epilogue

So what in the world does one take away from a book like this?

My hope is some of you who find yourself in the ditch of life have been inspired by others who have been in the ditch to pick up the pieces and move forward with every fiber of your being. Maybe you are it the ditch because you did something stupid. Maybe you are in the ditch because you were not afraid to lose. And maybe you are there because it is just your plight to be there. The reason at this point really does not matter. What does matter is that you gather your papers, get them back in your basket, relentlessly move forward and never ever give up.

Maybe some of you have been inspired to take the time to look for folks God has put in your path who find themselves in the ditch. I hope you saw in the stories that most of the time you don't have to be a trained counselor or a person of wealth or power to help someone in the ditch. Sometimes a helping hand, a hand to hold or a listening ear does just fine.

If some of you have been motivated to abandon your defensive lifestyle to pursue excellence, this book will not have been written in vain. Hopefully, there will be more people willing to be the goat. More people willing to risk losing. More people willing to sacrifice. More people walking out in faith. And ultimately, more people living on a higher plane and realizing their purpose in life.

Maybe some have been reminded that life is short and the prize really is in the journey. You can live as one blown by the wind or you can live by intention as you engage people and squeeze all you can out of each moment.

Eulan Brown died in 1985 at the age of 46. I attended his funeral and even had the honor of being the funeral director in charge as we laid him to rest at Mount Olive Cemetery outside of Reynolds. Eulan would not have been surprised that only a few people showed up to pay their respects that day because he knew most folks didn't really know him.

He would be very surprised at how many folks know him now.

His life was a gift to us. His memory is now an inspiration to us.

His legacy is in the lessons he taught us.

Reynolds, Georgia

For those of you who have not been there, the city of Reynolds, Ga. is about halfway between Macon and Columbus. Reynolds was founded in 1853 and is said to be named in honor of John Reynolds, one of Georgia's famous governors. Some say it was named for L.C. Reynolds, Esquire and another source says it was named for the superintendent of the railroad at the time.

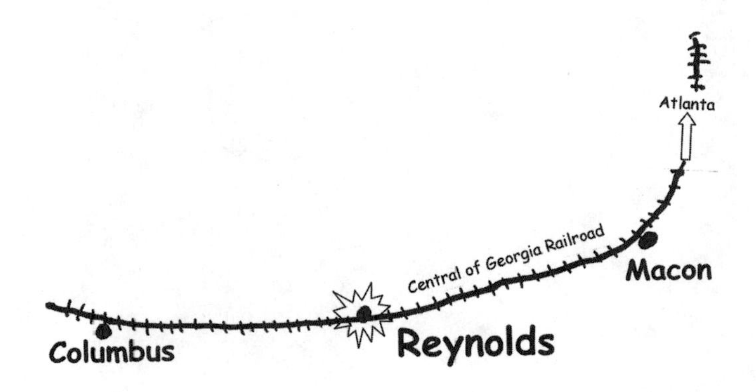

The building of the railroad was announced March 16, 1851 and brought change into the lives of the people. The railroad was left unfinished in the Beechwood swamp for a time, but with its completion Reynolds became a well laid out town, with symmetrical blocks 318 feet square and streets running north and south, east and west. One block was deeded to the new railroad site for the establishment of a depot area and a second was planned for a courthouse site. The Courthouse never came to fruition in Reynolds, and after a time, the lot originally designated for the Courthouse was made the church park with the Methodist Church on one corner and the Baptist Church on the other.